ACKNOWLEDGEMENTS:

This special edition of **The Long Journey** has been made possible through a generous financial contribution from:
THE STATE OF KUWAIT

and additional financial support from:
The OPEC Fund for International Development
Kosei-Kai Fund for Peace, Japan

Contents

Introduction		**3**
1948-1966	The exodus. UNRWA brings relief aid to refugees.	**5**
	"The choice is between saving the lives of many thousands of people or permitting them to die."	
1967-1981	The 1967 war. UNRWA again helps refugees rebuild their lives.	**29**
	...an "overwhelming sense of bewilderment and shock was felt by the inhabitants of the areas affected by the hostilities as the cataclysm swept over them."	
1982-1986	Crises in Lebanon. UNRWA delivers emergency aid; continues services in other fields.	**49**
	"Tens of thousands of Palestine refugees were made homeless once again and were reduced to a state of misery."	
1987-1995	The *intifadah*. The Israel-PLO Declaration of Principles. UNRWA starts Peace Implementation Programme.	**65**
	"There is a growing sense of despair and hopelessness among the refugees..."	

Previous page:
A Palestine refugee woman cut off from her home by the "Green Line" - the armistice line established after the 1948 Arab-Israeli war.

Introduction

BY UNRWA COMMISSIONER-GENERAL **ILTER TÜRKMEN**

The Palestine question is almost contemporary with the United Nations. The United Nations was created in 1945 and the General Assembly adopted the Palestine resolution in 1947. The Arab-Israeli war started in 1948 and since then the United Nations has been deeply involved with the fate of the Palestinian people. As a matter of fact, historically the United Nations has never had a commitment to a people to the extent of its commitment to the Palestinians. It has never provided systematic assistance to one people for such a long time.

The United Nations has had, throughout its 50 years, a considerable number of successes. UNRWA, which marked its 45th anniversary in May 1995, surely ranks as one of the most successful humanitarian assistance operations in the history of the United Nations. It has provided, throughout this period, essential education, health and relief and social services to a Palestine refugee population which now numbers over three million people. Thousands of Palestinians have been educated in UNRWA schools, received health care in UNRWA clinics, obtained humanitarian assistance to keep them from destitution, and benefited from the social services provided by the Agency. Now, as Palestinians in the West Bank and Gaza Strip assume more and more control over their daily lives, UNRWA, as part of the United Nations, is taking steps to support the peace process and is working towards the day when it will eventually be able to hand over its operations.

The United Nations record of action towards the Palestinians is a source of pride. It has helped the Palestinians to maintain their identity and their culture and has constituted an indispensable element of political and social stability in the area over a turbulent half-century. It has, to the extent possible, alleviated the hardship, indignity and suffering caused by more than 25 years of occupation.

It is therefore with pride that I present to you this unique photographic essay which gives an insight into the lives of Palestine refugees and the work of the Agency through the lenses of UNRWA photographers and through pictures on loan from the United Nations archives. "The Long Journey" has been envisaged as a historic document, published on the occasion of the 45th anniversary of UNRWA, to pay tribute to the Agency's staff and the people at the centre of this human tragedy - the Palestine refugees.

Ilter Türkmen

"The choice is between saving the lives of many thousands of people or permitting them to die."

48-66

"Give birth to me again
Give birth to me again that I may know
in which land I will die, in which land
I will come to life again"

Mahmoud Darwish, Palestinian poet

By the tens of thousands they fled. North to Lebanon and the Syrian Arab Republic. South to Gaza. East to Arab Palestine or on to Jordan.

"The choice is between saving the lives of many thousands of people or permitting them to die," said Count Folke Bernadotte, the UN Mediator for Palestine, in a report issued the day before he was assassinated.

This was the situation in September 1948 after years of missions, talks, the British Mandate in Palestine, frequent violence, Zionist aspirations fostered by the treatment of Jews in Europe, a partition resolution passed by the United Nations and the establishment of the State of Israel in May 1948.

Palestinians began fleeing in late 1947 but the bulk of them left or were driven from their homes between April and August 1948. By the autumn of 1948 a humanitarian disaster of immense proportions had taken shape, with more than 700,000 Palestinians in flight. It had the effect of tripling the population of Gaza, doubling that of the west bank of the Jordan River and raising the population of the area east of the river by 20 per cent. The influx imposed a heavy burden on the countries to which the refugees fled, countries which were far from rich themselves.

The lives of the refugees were turned upside down. They were faced with disease, lack of food and water, life in unfamiliar places and overcrowding. They lost homes, farms, family, their lives. Many were crowded into refugee camps in tents. Others lived in caves or in the open.

The refugees hoped they would soon be able to return to their homes. UN General Assembly resolutions called for their return or compensation for losses. But as there was no way to enforce these resolutions, the refugees remained destitute.

The United Nations responded in 1948 by creating the United Nations Relief for Palestine Refugees (UNRPR), which coordinated the relief work of UN specialized agencies and non-governmental organizations, including the International Committee of the Red Cross and the American Friends Service Committee.

An Economic Survey Mission established by the United Nations Conciliation Commission for Palestine (UNCCP) urged public works projects, afforestation, road construction and the development of water resources. Some projects were launched, but there was never enough money committed to bring the plans to full fruition. There was also political opposition to integrating the refugees into the host countries. The Mission foresaw the termination of UN relief aid to Palestine refugees by the end of 1950, with the public works programme continuing through June 1951.

When it became clear that the Palestine refugee issue was not going to be resolved quickly, the General Assembly created the United Nations Relief and Works Agency for Palestine Refugees in the Near East (UNRWA). The founding resolution was passed in December 1949, and UNRWA started its operations in May 1950, taking over the assets of UNRPR including 64 schools and 46 clinics, Although it was originally conceived as a temporary agency, UNRWA has had its mandate renewed regularly over the past 45 years.

During its initial one-year mandate, UNRWA tried to alleviate the misery faced by the refugees. Medical services were provided, schools were set up in the sand and efforts begun to replace tents with better shelters.

Palestinian families evacuate Al-Falouja village, leaving behind their homes, olive trees, ploughed tracts of land and planted fields.

In addition to providing food rations to refugees, the Agency established supplementary feeding programmes for the young and the ill to ensure that they had the necessary minimum daily nutrition.

In the political arena, Jordan annexed the West Bank in 1950, while the Gaza Strip was administered by Egypt.

UNRWA had its headquarters in Beirut, with field offices in Damascus, Gaza and Jerusalem. In the early days, the Government of Switzerland provided the Agency with a small plane which made possible quick contact between headquarters and field offices.

As most refugees tried to rebuild some semblance of a normal life, the Gaza Strip remained a special case. Because of its poverty, lack of infrastructure and isolation from its natural trading hinterland, it was considered in the Commissioner-General`s 1954/55 Annual Report "a unique area in the Agency`s operation."

The absence of job opportunities for some 300,000 persons inevitably affected morale. While the authorities were generally able to maintain order, there were occasional outbreaks of violence in February 1955.

In 1951, up to 87 per cent of refugees living in camps were housed in tents. By 1954, that proportion had dropped to 32 per cent and by the end of 1955 tents had been replaced in most areas of UNRWA`s operations by either prefabricated shelters or cinder block dwellings. Other programmes of education and health care were being developed and life had settled down to relative normalcy, if life as a refugee could be called normal.

Then in 1956, the Middle East was again shaken by violence. Israel invaded Egypt while France and Britain landed troops at Port Said in the Suez Canal. On 1 November, Israel occupied the Gaza Strip, an occupation which lasted until March 1957, when the Egyptian administration was restored. Almost 400 Gazans were killed, UNRWA supply lines were cut, curfews were imposed, Agency services were disrupted and food supplies were looted.

The May 1958 political crisis and subsequent events in Lebanon again hampered the work of UNRWA. With ports closed and roads between Beirut and Damascus cut, UNRWA had great difficulty supplying its fields in Syria and Jordan. It took a year to resume full operations.

Nine years after UNRWA was established, it was time to take a fresh look at the Agency's role. UN Secretary-General Dag Hammarskjöld did this in a report to the General Assembly in 1959. He made the point that integration of refugees in the host countries would not be possible if it were brought about by forcing people into new positions against their will.

In his report, the Secretary-General stated, "I strongly and unreservedly recommend the continuance of the United Nations activities in support of the refugees...." His report and recommendations formed the basis for a General Assembly Resolution in December 1959 extending UNRWA's mandate for three years. The resolution also directed the Agency to expand its programme of self-support and vocational training in order to enable the refugees to acquire the skills they needed to find jobs in their new environment. Many of the refugees were from rural areas and did not have the skills to earn a living in an urban setting.

With additional funding injected into the Agency during the World Refugee Year (1959/60), UNRWA was able to expand its vocational and technical training programmes from 580 training places in 1960 to 2,130 in 1964. One of the new training centres opened was the Ramallah Women's Training Centre, the first of its kind in the Middle East. In addition, UNRWA increased the number of university scholarships for young refugees.

During the 1960's, UNRWA also expanded its health programme, especially in the area of mother and child care. The Agency pioneered the use of oral rehydration salts on a mass scale, a life-saving method now used throughout the world by UNICEF.

By the end of 1966, the refugee population had grown to more than 1.3 million. Although always hard-pressed financially, UNRWA was able to improve the health of refugees, provide social assistance to the neediest and equip the younger generation with marketable skills. Meanwhile, education and skills-training took over from relief as UNRWA's major programme. Thousands of young Palestinians found jobs locally or in the Gulf area, helping to build the Arab world.

The cessation of hostilities in the Middle East lasted nearly a decade, but events soon took a dramatic turn that would change the face of the region.

Gaza desert, December 1949. A convoy of trucks and cars, led by white UN jeeps, travels through the desert carrying refugees and their belongings from Gaza to Hebron in what was then Transjordan, the place from which they had fled during the time of the 1948 war.

Chronology

1922 League of Nations approves British Mandate over Palestine.

1939 Britain proposes an independent Palestine in 10 years.

1947 UN Special Committee on Palestine (UNSCOP), established in May, recommends the division of Palestine into an Arab state, a Jewish state and the city of Jerusalem linked in an economic union. Independence foreseen within two years.

General Assembly adopts partition resolution on 29 November. Arab Governments reject the plan.

1948 British Mandate ends on 15 May. Israel proclaims independence one day before.

Between April and August, more than 700,000 people flee their homes in Palestine and become refugees.

UN Mediator for Palestine Count Folke Bernadotte assassinated on 17 September, soon after his appointment.

General Assembly establishes United Nations Relief for Palestine Refugees (UNRPR).

General Assembly adopts resolution 194 on 11 December recognizing Palestine refugees' right of return or compensation and establishing the UN Conciliation Commission for Palestine (UNCCP).

1949 UNCCP sets up Economic Survey Mission. UN General Assembly adopts resolution 302 (IV) on 8 December establishing UNRWA. UNRWA takes over assets of UNRPR.

Jordan annexes West Bank. UNRWA begins operations on 1 May with relief accounting for 69 per cent of its budget.	**1950**
UNRWA opens first vocational training centres in Kalandia and Gaza.	**1954**

Israel attacks Egypt, occupying the Gaza Strip.	**1956**
Last Israeli troops leave Gaza on 7 March.	**1957**
Political crisis in Lebanon.	**1958**

UN Secretary-General Dag Hammarskjöld recommends continuing UN aid for Palestine refugees.	**1959**

First mass use of oral rehydration salts pioneered by UNRWA. UNRWA opens teacher training centre for men in Ramallah near Jerusalem, Wadi Seer Vocational Training Centre in Jordan (1960), Damascus Vocational Training Centre in the Syrian Arab Republic (1961), Ramallah Women's Training Centre and Siblin Training Centre in Lebanon (1962).	**1960-62**
UNRWA/UNESCO Institute of Education set up to carry out in-service teacher training.	**1964**

Registered refugee population surpasses 1.3 million. UNRWA schools accommodate 175,900 pupils and health centres register 4,5 million patient visits during the year.	**1966**

Nahr el-Bared refugee camp, Tripoli, Lebanon, 1952. This was the daily reality for thousands of refugees who lost homes, land and livelihoods in the Arab-Israeli war. Six thousand people lived in this camp.

Previous pages:
Last days in Jaffa, 1948. Barefoot and pushing their belongings in prams and carts, Arab families leave the Mediterranean coastal town of Jaffa which became part of the greater Tel Aviv area, Israel.

Two generations made refugees. A girl soothes her grandfather as he rests on a sackcloth pillow during their journey from northern Galilee to the relative safety of a refugee camp in Lebanon.

Mieh Mieh camp, south Lebanon: Some refugees had nowhere else to live but in disused barracks where sackcloth curtains gave the only semblance of privacy.

Facing old age with only a canvas roof to call home. After the Arab-Israeli war, refugees found shelter wherever they could, living in tents and even in caves.

Making do. Women help build a makeshift shelter out of branches.

Jebel Joffeh, Amman, Jordan - a place of refuge for thousands who fled in the 1948 war. Stones and drums keep the corrugated iron roofs from blowing away during harsh winter storms.

Facing page:
Bowed but not broken. This couple in Nahr el-Bared camp, Lebanon, straighten out their tent again after winter storms blew it down and turned the earth into mud.

Overleaf:
UNRWA provided one good meal nearly every day for children at its network of supplementary feeding centres such as this one at Dbayeh camp near Beirut, Lebanon.

Father and daughter pack rations to take home after collecting them at an UNRWA distribution point in Aqaba in southern Jordan. UNRWA issued basic rations to thousands of families for many years.

Schools in the sand, Khan Younis, Gaza. The first UNRWA schools were in tents or in the open air. UNRWA started out with 93 schools and more than 35,000 pupils in 1950.

Barefoot on the rocks. A new day starts with exercises at an UNRWA school.

Right from the beginning, UNRWA welcomed girls into its schools. In 1950, 27% of the Agency's pupils were girls. By 1966, they already made up 41% of the school population.

Facing page:
Education: hope for a better future. Men who had missed out on schooling learn alongside boys at an UNRWA school. Education soon became UNRWA's largest programme.

U.N.R.W.A.P.R
WORKS RELIEF PROJECTS
MACHINE WORKSHOP
ESTABLISHED UNDER REINTEGRATION PROGRAMME

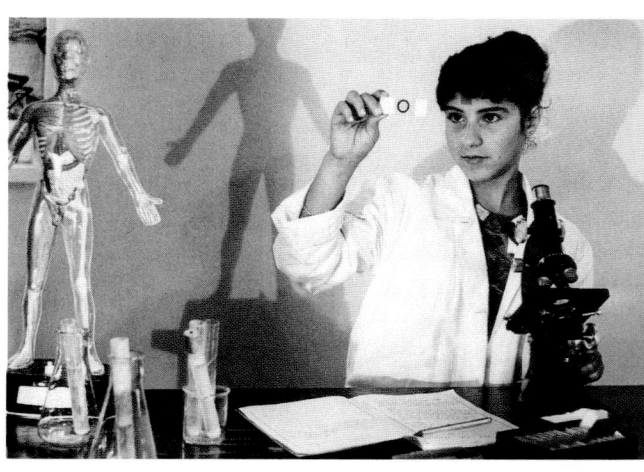

UNRWA opened up opportunities for refugee women, thousands of whom became teachers - many in Agency schools - after completing UNRWA's teacher training courses. Here, a trainee teacher takes part in a science lesson at Ramallah Women's Training Centre near Jerusalem.

Graduation day. Ahmed Dahsheh (centre) was hired by the Government of Bahrain as a teacher of English almost immediately after completing training at UNRWA's Siblin training centre, near Saida in Lebanon.

Learning for a profession. Two students on a land surveying course at UNRWA's Kalandia Vocational Training Centre near Jerusalem. Nearly 50,000 Palestine refugees have graduated from the Agency's eight vocational training centres. Many have gone on to find highly responsible jobs.

Pioneers. Mrs. In'am Mufti, the first Principal of UNRWA's Ramallah Women's Training Centre, with some of her students. RWTC was the first institution in the Middle East to offer teacher training and vocational courses for refugee women.

Facing page:
Youngsters concentrate hard as they learn a trade at UNRWA's
Amman Training Centre, Jordan.

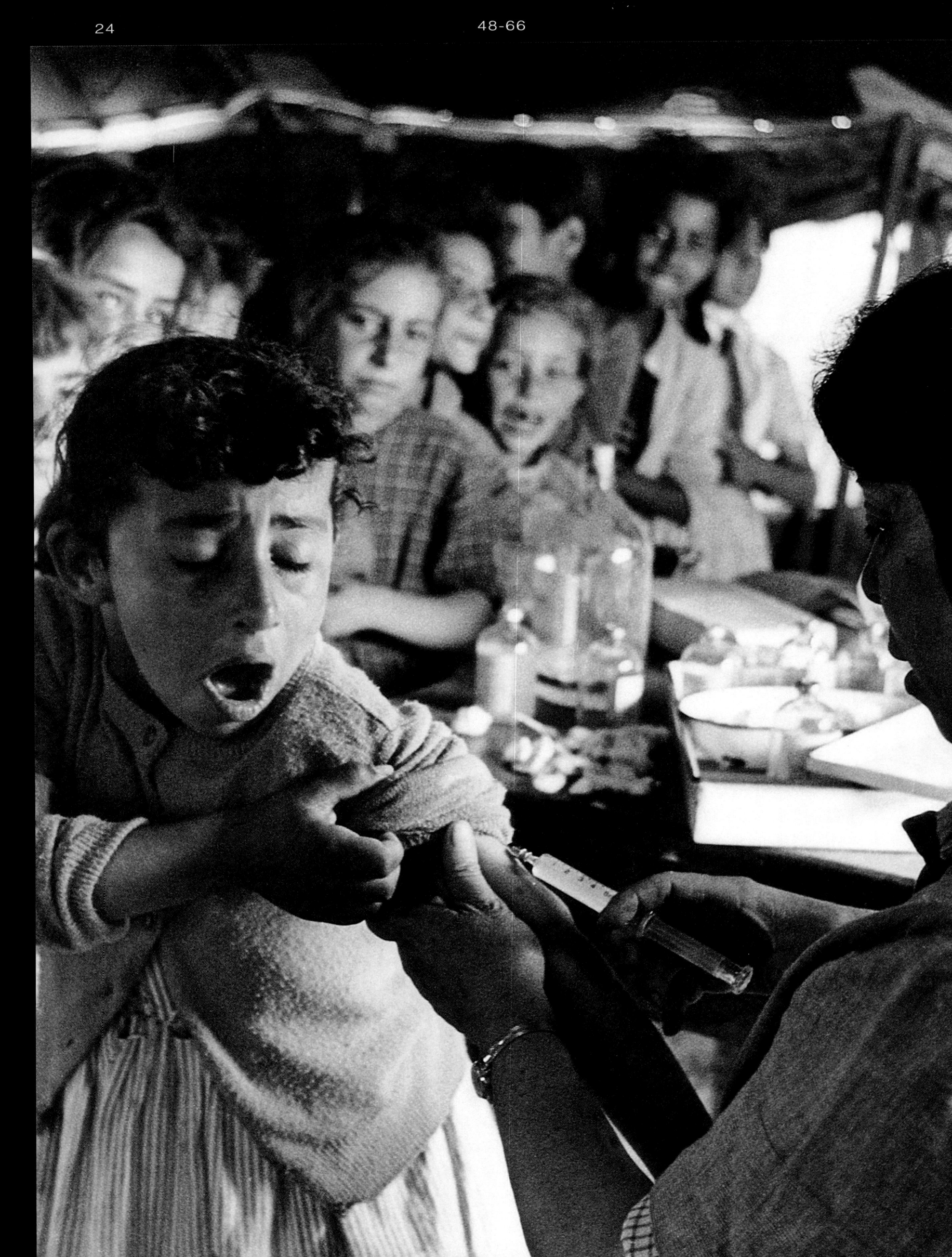

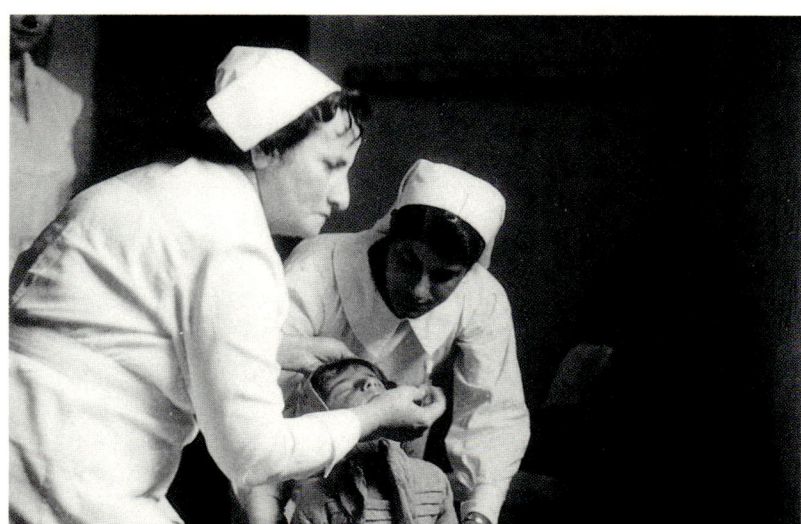

In one of the first clinics set up by UNRWA, two nurses give emergency aid to a child.

Medical care. A mother and her child receive medical care from a doctor at an UNRWA clinic in Khan Eshieh camp near Damascus in the Syrian Arab Republic. The Agency has continued to provide a good, basic health service, with emphasis on preventive and mother-and-child care.

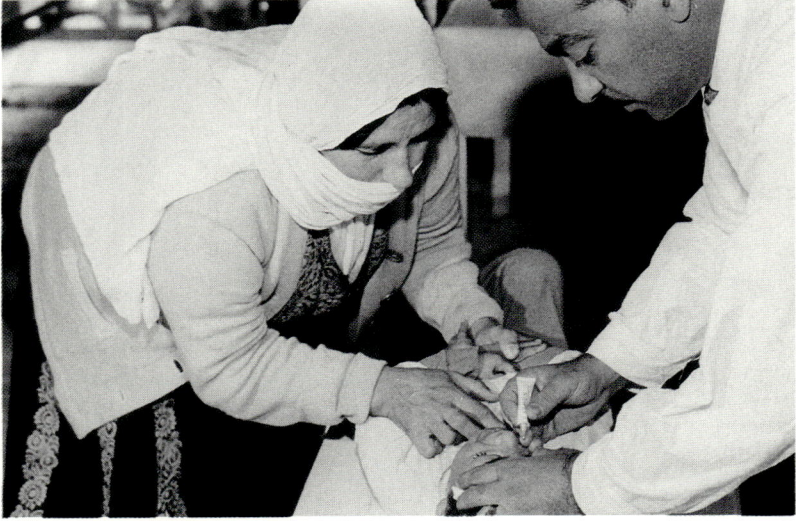

At an UNRWA clinic, a child receives treatment for an eye complaint- a frequent problem in the dusty environment.

Facing page:
Ouch! A girl lines up with her classmates for a vaccination in a refugee camp near Amman, Jordan. UNRWA has had great success with its immunization programme, controlling many diseases and helping to keep the Palestine refugees healthy.

New buildings. As time went on, and no solution was found to the refugees' plight, UNRWA replaced tents with basic shelters and constructed proper school buildings - such as this one in Beach camp, Gaza.

Keys. Hands reach forward to receive from an UNRWA official the keys to the new shelters at Aida camp, Bethlehem.

Tents and shelters. In Aida camp, a refugee tries the keys to his new shelter built alongside his old tent.

The evening sun casts long shadows over Khan Younis camp in the Gaza Strip.

...An "overwhelming sense of bewilderment and shock was felt by the inhabitants of the areas affected by the hostilities as the cataclysm swept over them."

67-81

By the tens of thousands they fled, many for a second time. From Gaza and the West Bank across the Jordan River to Jordan. From the Golan Heights area, northwards into Syria. Still others fled to Lebanon.

"No factual and necessarily brief account can, however, portray the overwhelming sense of bewilderment and shock felt by the inhabitants of the areas affected by the hostilities as the cataclysm swept over them. The disruption of the lives and careers of countless persons... the personal tragedies resulting from the separation of husbands and wives, parents and children, are only some of the problems which confront so many of the former Arab inhabitants of Palestine." This is how the Commissioner-General`s Annual Report of 1966/67 described the impact of the June 1967 Arab-Israeli war.

After hostilities broke out on 6 June 1967 between Israel and neighbouring Arab states, about 150,000 registered refugees fled from the West Bank into Jordan. Another 38,500 fled to Jordan from the Gaza Strip. Some 16,000 registered refugees from the Golan/ Quneitra area fled mainly to Damascus and Dera´a. Refugees for a second time. Another 335,000 people were displaced.

Refugee camps around Jericho were almost totally emptied; nine new emergency camps were set up in Jordan and Syria. Tents sprang up amidst the arid landscape again. It would take UNRWA another seven years to replace these tents with more solid shelters.

Even a year later, many thousands of refugees and displaced people were still in need of the essentials for physical survival - food, water, shelter, blankets, clothing and basic health care. An exceptionally harsh, rainy winter brought additional suffering. Residents of the West Bank and Gaza Strip were subjected to the difficulties of living under an occupying authority.

An exchange of letters between UNRWA and Israel enabled the Agency to continue its operations in the occupied territory. With the occupation of East Jerusalem and the West Bank, UNRWA had to open a new Field Office in Amman to care for refugees living in Jordan.

The occupation weakened an already stagnant economy in the Gaza Strip. There was fertile ground for unrest among the population, more than two-thirds of whom were refugees. Strikes and violent incidents became almost a permanent feature of life. A climax was reached in mid-1971 when 16,000 refugees were displaced by the demolition of their homes by Israeli authorities on security grounds.

Over the next few years, the focus shifted north. In the October 1973 Arab-Israeli conflict, thousands of refugees were displaced by fighting. Supply lines in Lebanon and Syria were interrupted and UNRWA`s programmes were disrupted.

Facing page:
Allenby Bridge, June 1967. They fled war again, this time on foot, carrying the sick, the old and the frail and their few belongings on their backs, across the demolished Allenby Bridge into east Jordan. The land behind them fell under Israeli military control for more than 25 years.

Israeli air raids and incursions into southern Lebanon caused continuous flows of refugees north and then back south throughout the next decade. One air raid in 1974 completely destroyed Nabatieh refugee camp in south Lebanon.

With the outbreak of the Lebanese civil war in 1975, UNRWA activities throughout the country were often hampered and sometimes even briefly paralyzed. Two Palestine refugee camps in Beirut - Jisr el-Basha and Tel el-Za`tar - were destroyed in the fighting which killed many and displaced over 10,000 refugees. The situation in 1976 became so acute that UNRWA was forced to temporarily move its headquarters from Beirut to Amman and Vienna.

March 1978 brought an Israeli military operation in south Lebanon during which some 67,000 refugees fled their homes.

UNRWA`s short-lived return to Beirut in November 1977 ended in the summer of 1978, when the Agency was again forced to leave Beirut for Amman and Vienna. Parts of headquarters are still in the two cities, with a move of the Vienna headquarters to the area of operations foreseen for 1995/96.

While most UNRWA services continued relatively normally in other fields, the Agency had to mount a number of emergency operations in Lebanon to provide food, water, shelter and emergency health care for the Palestine refugees there. At the same time, the Agency faced continued financial crises which threatened its very existence and especially its education programme in Jordan. Pared expenditure, coupled with emergency contributions, enabled the Agency to carry on providing its normal education, health and relief and social services to the refugee population.

Destruction, Qalqilya 1967. One reason why they fled. Many homes in frontier villages like Qalqilya were damaged or totally destroyed in the 1967 Arab-Israeli war.

Chronology

War breaks out between Israel and neighbouring Arab States on 5 June.

Israel occupies East Jerusalem on 6 June and, soon after, the West Bank, the Gaza Strip, the Golan Heights and the Sinai Peninsula.

Thousands of Palestinians, including many UNRWA-registered refugees, flee from the West Bank and Gaza Strip to Jordan. UNRWA begins emergency aid programme.

1967

UNRWA begins replacing tents in emergency camps with more permanent shelters.

1968

Unrest in Jordan and Gaza. Agency services disrupted. General Assembly sets up working group on UNRWA finances to deal with Agency's financial crisis.

1969-72

Renewed Arab-Israeli hostilities.

1973

Nabatieh camp, recently rebuilt by UNRWA in south Lebanon, destroyed in Israeli air raid.

1974

UNRWA completes replacement of tents in emergency camps. Fighting breaks out in Lebanon.
UNRWA headquarters forced to leave Beirut. Two refugee camps in Beirut destroyed in fighting.

1975-76

Israeli incursion into south Lebanon displaces some 67,000 refugees. UNRWA provides emergency aid.

1978

Registered refugee population reaches 1.9 million, with 321,000 pupils enrolled in UNRWA schools and 4.5 million patient visits at UNRWA clinics.

1981

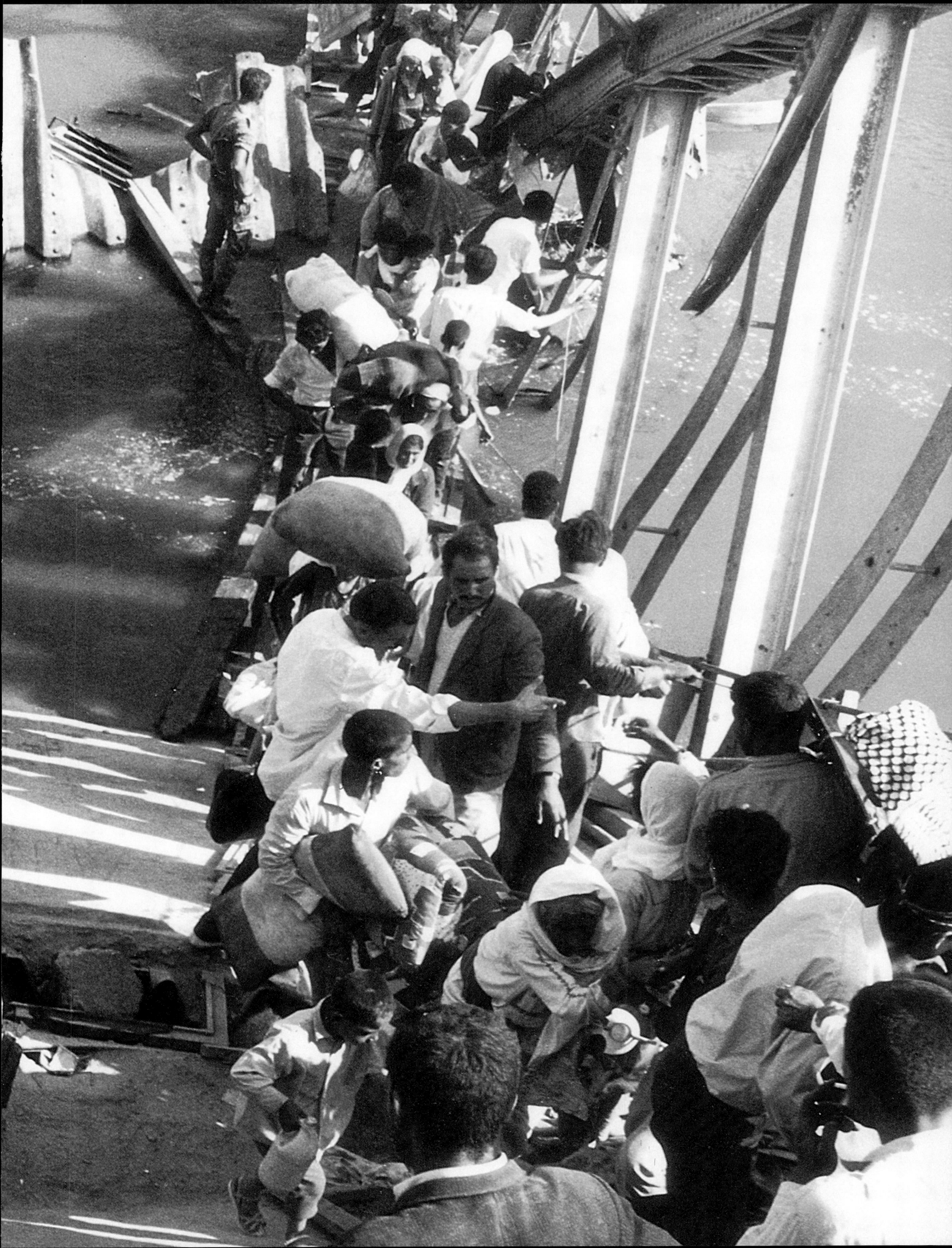

Previous pages:
The Bridge - symbol of the 1967 war. About 400,000 Palestinians fled across the Jordan River to escape the second Arab-Israeli conflict. Many fled across this bridge from the West Bank and Gaza.

Tent city. 3,000 homeless refugees sheltered in Jaramana camp in Syria following the 1967 war. They were among 10,000 refugees given shelter in four camps in Syria.

Exhausted by the burdens of refugee life, a woman seeks out sleep in her tent.

Anxiety became one of the few constant factors in the disrupted lives of thousands of refugees. Throughout the turmoil, UNRWA continued to provide emergency relief aid and regular education, health, relief and social services.

Bewildered Palestinians on the road near Souf camp in Jordan after the 1967 war. Thousands of refugees, registered with UNRWA after the 1948 war, had to flee again in 1967. Also on the move were thousands of other Palestinians who were displaced for the first time.

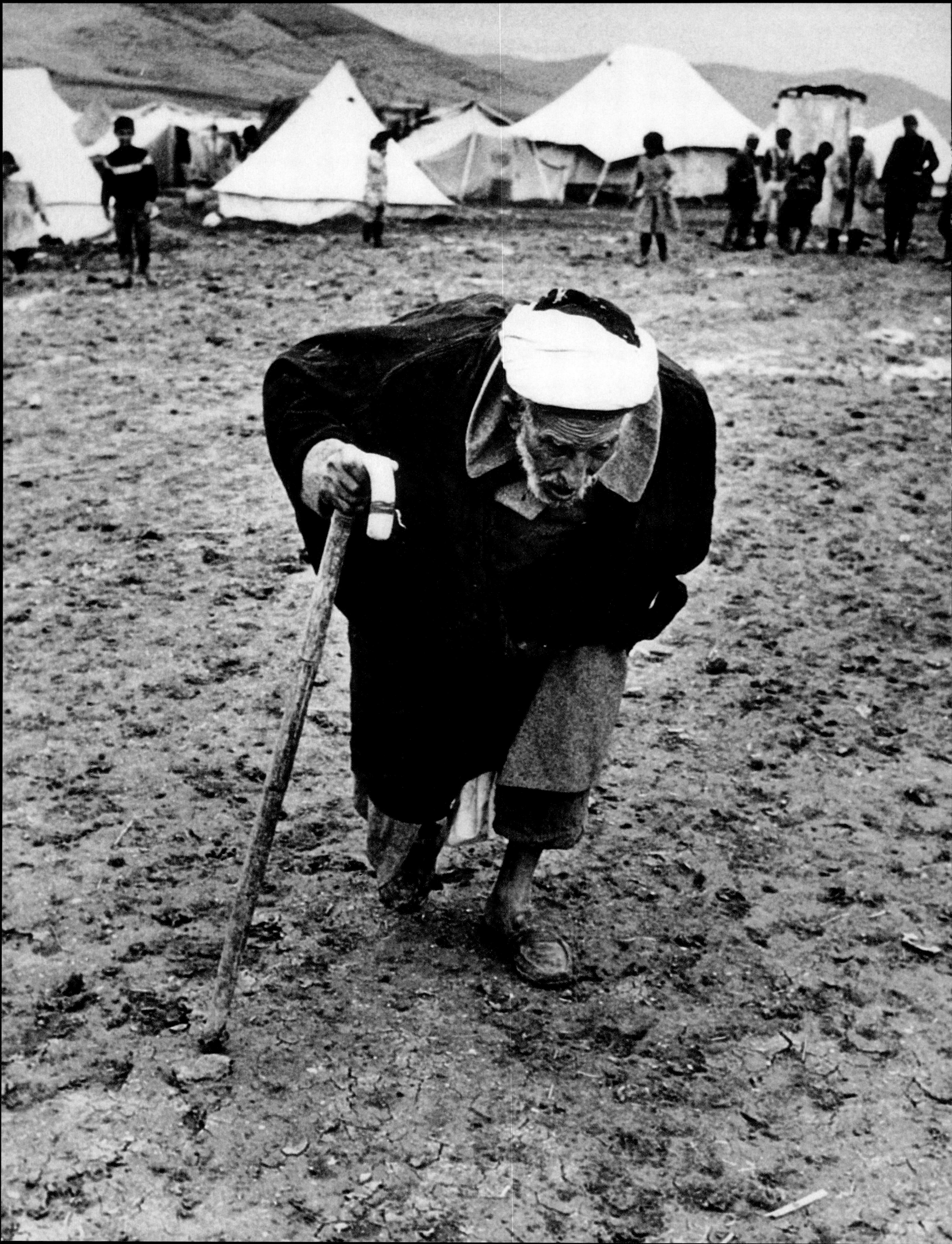

UNRWA workers distribute food rations to help women keep their families alive.

Colleagues from UNRWA's health service at Marka emergency camp line up for a photo, 1969. In the background - the camp, where some of the tents have already been replaced with prefabricated shelters.

School days to remember. By 1981, 321,000 children were attending UNRWA schools.

Facing page:
Facing misery in his later years, an elderly refugee trudges through the dried mud in Baqa'a camp, Jordan.

Baqa'a camp, in the hills north of Amman, Jordan was one of six camps set up in east Jordan to accommodate thousands of refugees and displaced persons from the West Bank and Gaza, occupied during the June 1967 Arab-Israeli- war. Today the camp houses more than 70,000 people.

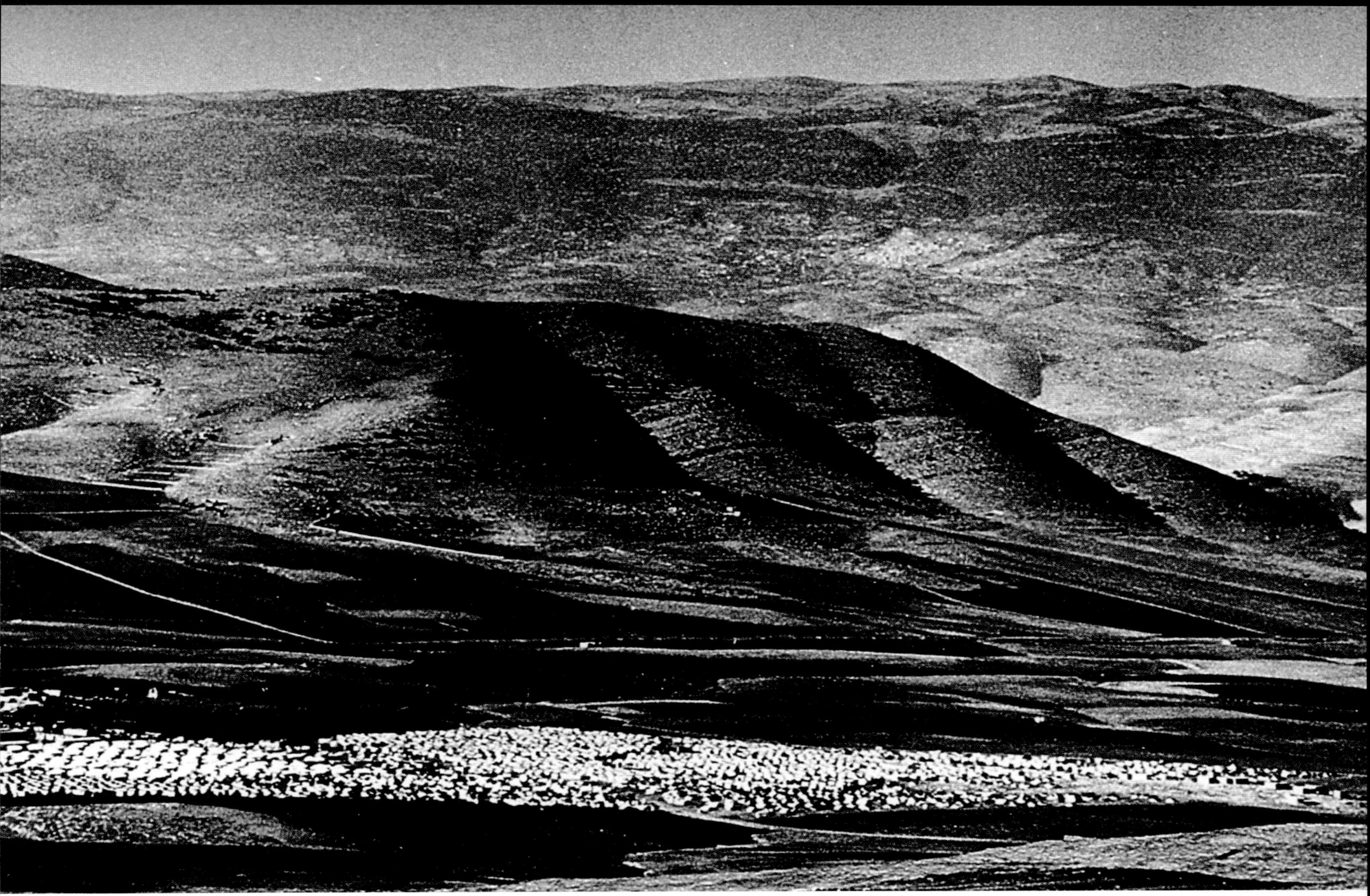

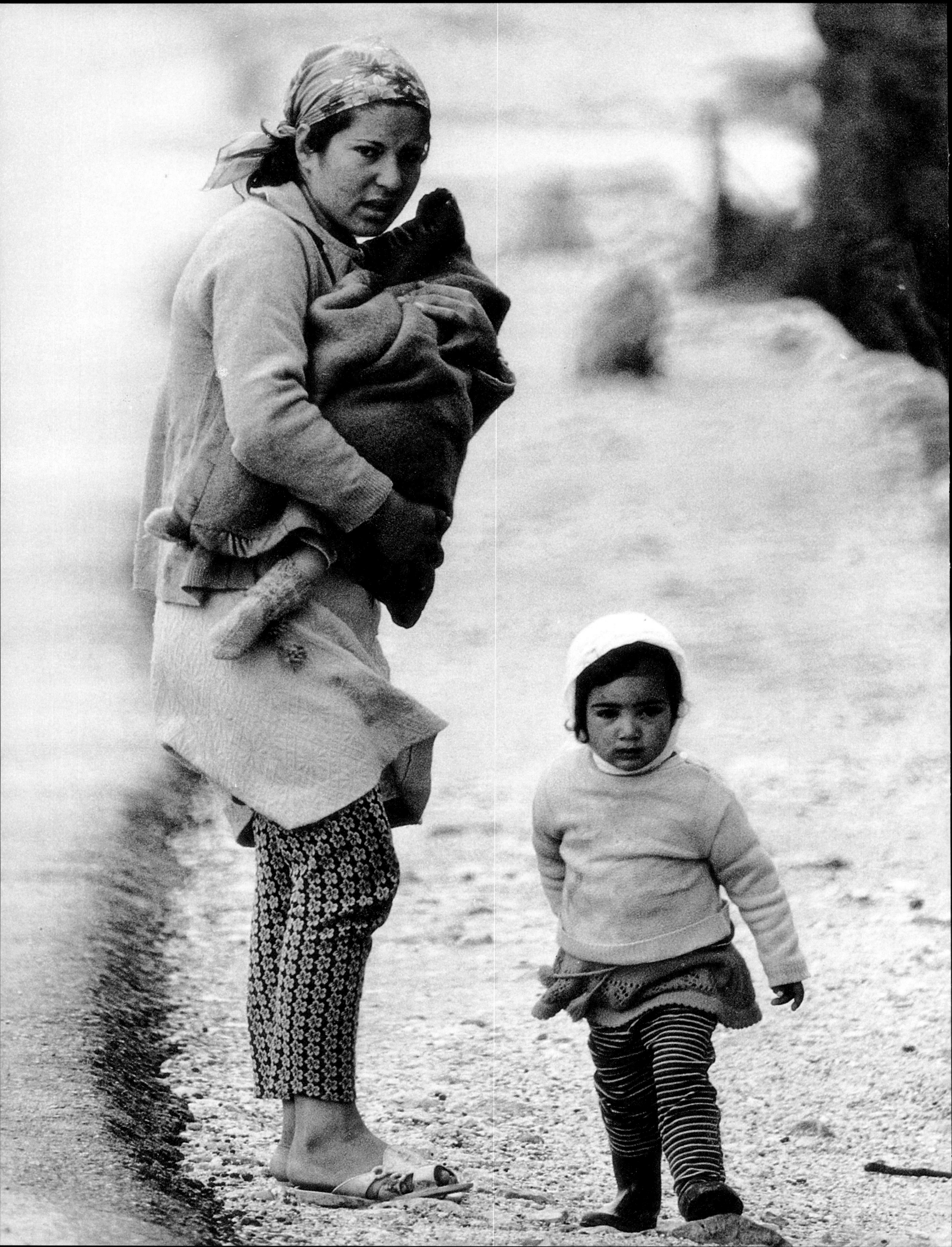

A crowded UNRWA health centre in a refugee camp. Agency clinics concentrate on preventive and mother-and-child health care.

Refugees, some of them UNRWA workers, collect bags of flour at an UNRWA distribution centre in the ancient city of Karak, Jordan.

A school teacher in Karameh in Jordan gets an enthusiastic response from his class. Refugees have traditionally shown great enthusiasm for education, seeing it as their best chance to secure a better future.

Pupils in Baqa'a camp, Jordan, help arrange books and periodicals destined for school libraries in the camp. Due to severe financial constraints, there were only one or two books per pupil in UNRWA schools.

Facing page:
Dheisheh camp, Bethlehem. Harsh winters added to the refugees' plight.

Her husband killed, youngest son wounded and home destroyed in the 16 May 1974 attack on Nabatieh camp, south Lebanon, a 1948 refugee (right), shelters in the camp's mosque.

Nabatieh camp for Palestine refugees, destroyed by an Israeli air raid, 1974.

Bulldozed. Some 16,000 Palestine refugees in the Gaza Strip were again displaced in the summer of 1971 when the occupation authorities destroyed their shelters so that roads could be built or widened for security purposes.

Beirut 1975. The shells of bombed-out buildings stand out starkly against the evening sky.

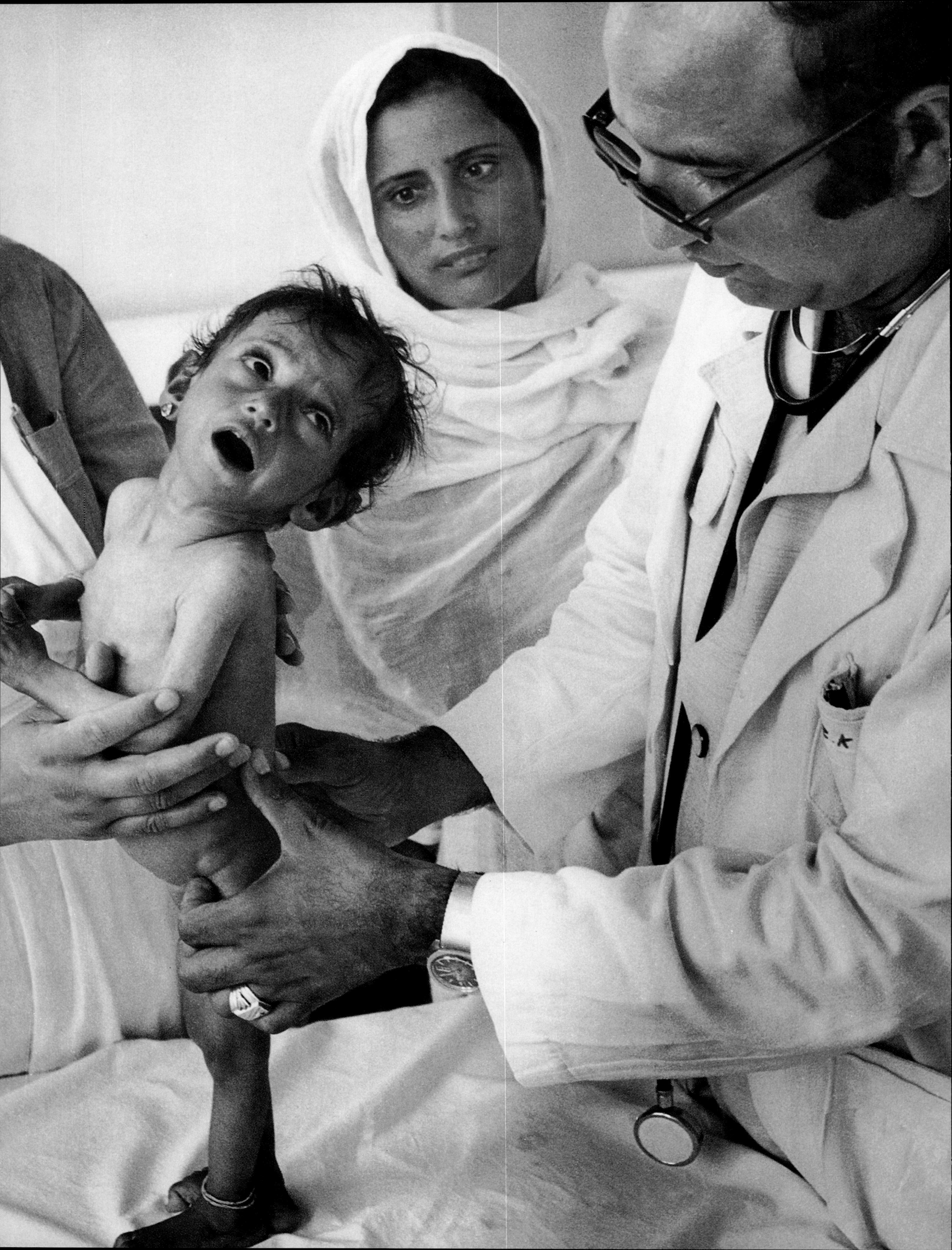

At UNRWA's Wadi Seer Vocational Training Centre in Amman, Jordan, women started taking courses which were previously considered suitable only for men. UNRWA has trained many Palestine refugee women in non-traditional fields such as engineering.

Dyeing wool to make rugs. People who fled to Gaza from the coastal towns brought with them a tradition of weaving, which was encouraged by UNRWA's early work programmes.

UNRWA's services go on: Instruction in electrical arc welding at UNRWA's vocational training centre in the Gaza Strip. Industrial development in the Arab countries increased the demand for technicians and skilled workers. UNRWA helped the refugees to take advantage of this opportunity by offering training.

Facing page:
Saving lives at an UNRWA dehydration/nutrition centre in Rafah camp, Gaza. This little girl was less than a year old when she was brought to an UNRWA clinic for treatment for severe dehydration. UNRWA pioneered the use of special salts, later used worldwide by UNICEF to combat diarrhoeal diseases.

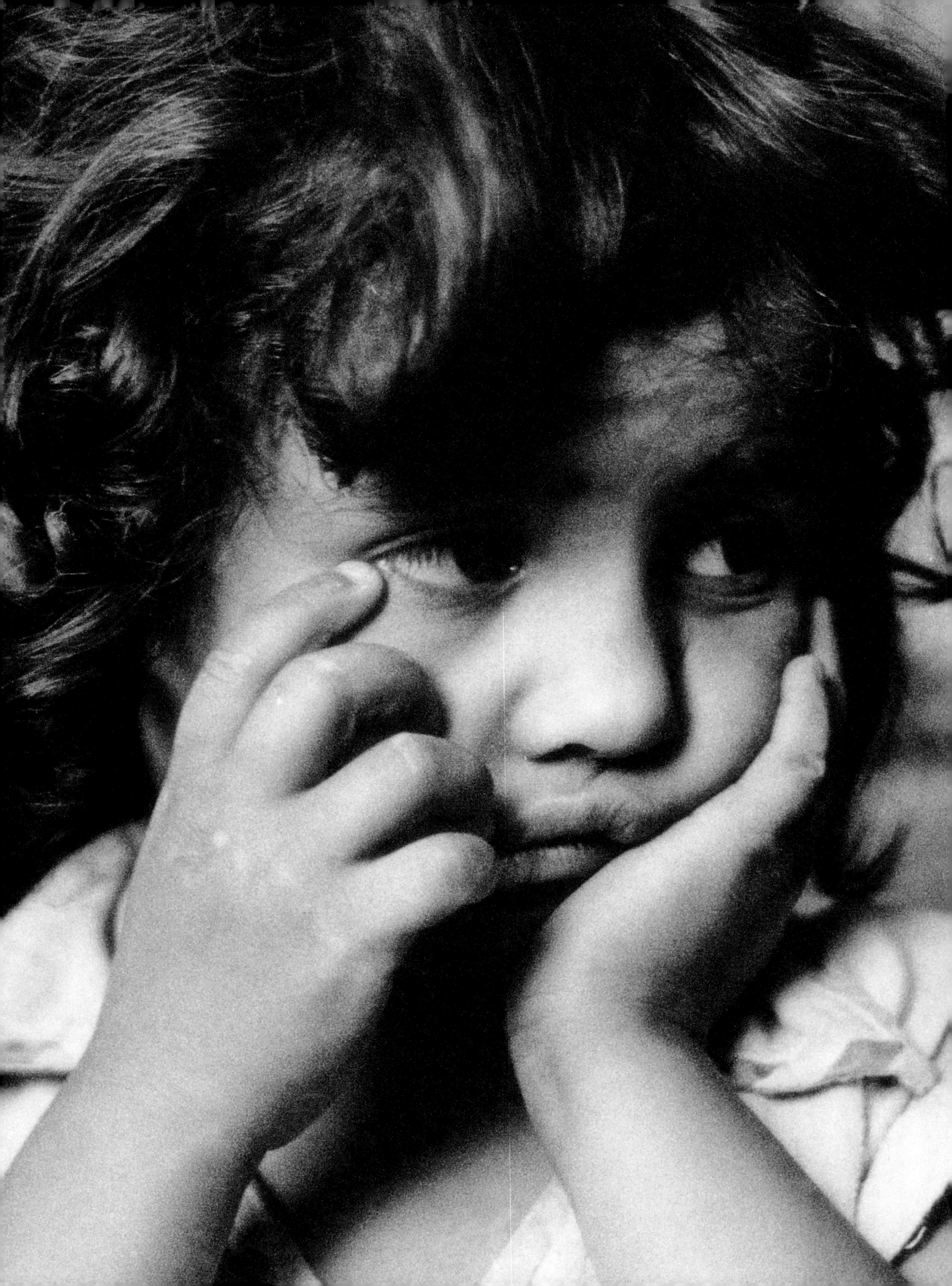

"Tens of thousands of Palestine refugees were made homeless once again and were reduced to a state of misery."

82-86

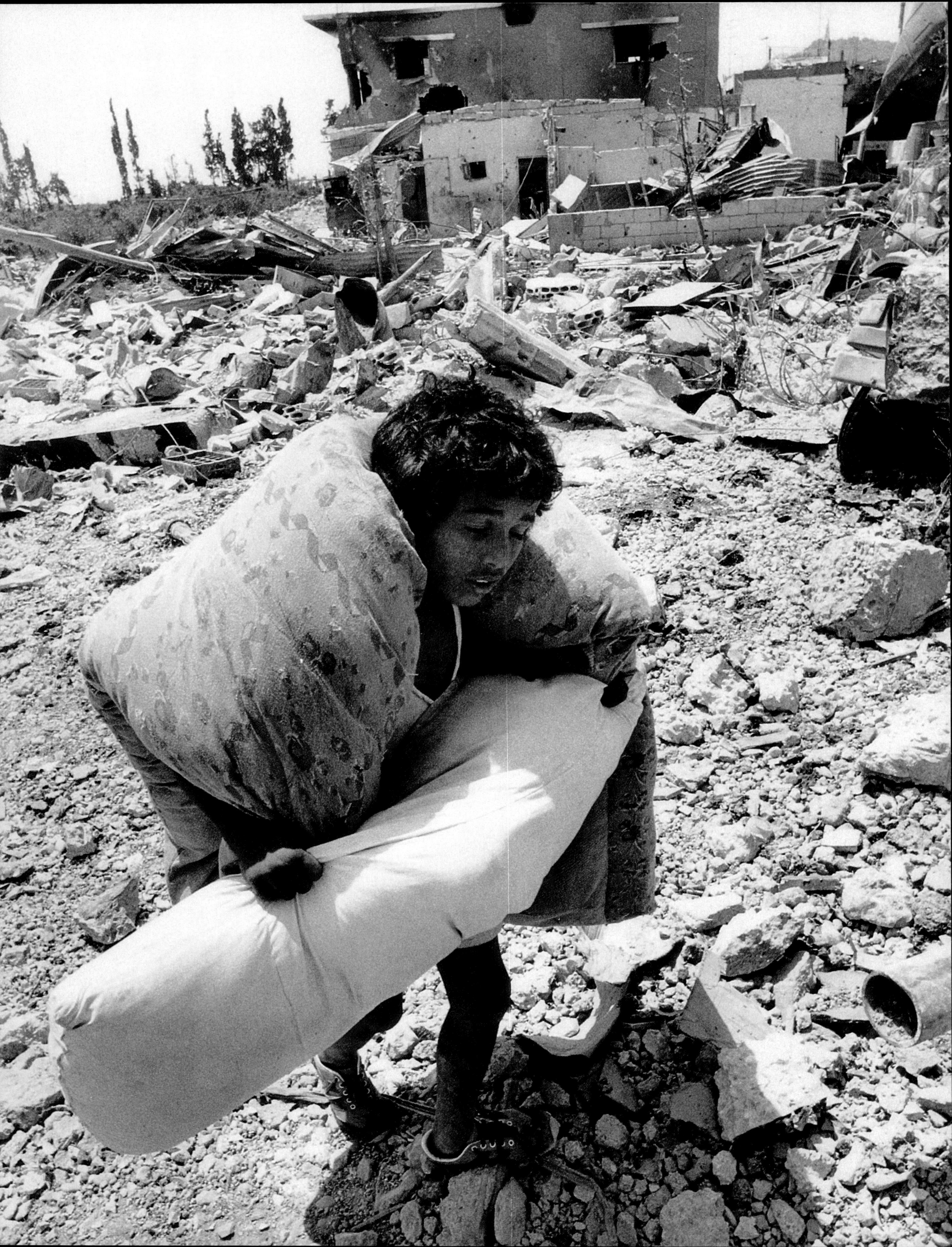

By the tens of thousands they fled. North to Beirut, Tripoli or the Beqa'a valley. East to Syria.

In early June 1982, Israel invaded Lebanon. "Tens of thousands of Palestine refugees were made homeless once more and were reduced to a state of misery. The condition of the families in many cases was made even worse by the absence of the menfolk who had been killed, wounded, taken prisoner or had retreated with units of the Palestine Liberation Army," said the Commissioner-General's Annual Report for the period 1981/82.

Of the 239,000 Palestine refugees registered with UNRWA in Lebanon, almost 200,000 were living in the areas most directly affected by the fighting. In eight refugee camps in Beirut, and the Saida and Tyre areas, 57 per cent of all refugee housing was destroyed with another 36 per cent damaged.

The Agency's $52 million emergency relief programme assisted 177,500 refugees including some 7,000 non-registered refugees. UNRWA provided food rations and once again set up tents, both to house the refugees and for use as schools, clinics and distribution centres. Because of the virtual siege of Beirut during the summer of 1982, aid for Palestinians in south Lebanon was provided via UNRWA's West Bank Field Office and for those in the Beqa'a valley from the Damascus Field Office.

To maintain vital food distribution for Palestinians in Lebanon, the Agency diverted food from the basic programme in other fields in 1982. As there were not adequate resources to resume the general distribution of rations, a new programme was introduced to provide food, small cash grants and other assistance to the poorest refugees, known as Special Hardship Cases (SHCs). The shift from general relief assistance to the SHC programme marked a major change in UNRWA's activities. By 1986 the relief activities comprised only 12 per cent of the Agency's regular budget.

Restoration of health services in south Lebanon was particularly difficult, as the network of clinics and hospitals run by the Palestine Red Crescent Society no longer existed. More medical staff were recruited and agreements were concluded with additional hospitals on a fee-for-service basis. By the end of 1982, all but three of the UNRWA schools in Lebanon were back in operation. This included schools operating out of 15 large tents at Ein el-Hilweh camp in Saida.

Rehousing the refugees was the biggest problem. Sites had to be cleared and water supply networks and sanitary facilities installed. Under a self-help system for housing rehabilitation, UNRWA provided 13,256 families with cash and/or building materials through June 1983.

The relief operation continued until March 1984, when both basic and emergency ration distributions ceased in Lebanon, although there were short-term emergency distributions at other times to relieve acute distress arising from the security situation.

The September 1982 massacre of several hundred Palestinians and other civilians in the Sabra quarter and Shatila camp in Beirut, dramatically exposed the vulnerability of Palestine refugees. Over the next several months, many Palestinians were killed in the Saida area and many others intimidated into leaving there homes in south Lebanon. The Commissioner-General issued several statements of concern and the Agency made representations to the responsible authorities, urging adequate measures for the protection of Palestine refugees.

The seemingly endless cycle of violence in Lebanon continued in subsequent years, especially in and around refugee camps in Beirut. The so-called "camps war" displaced about 18,000 refugees in the summer of 1985, necessitating another emergency relief programme. In September, heavy intra-Palestinian fighting broke out in the Tripoli area and lasted three weeks. Fighting resumed in Beirut in May 1986 with thousands fleeing again. Camps in south Lebanon, particularly Ein el-Hilweh, were subjected to repeated Israeli air raids. At the end of 1986, UNRWA was still providing assistance to some 33,000 displaced persons.

UNRWA's ability to continue to provide services to the refugees was increasingly threatened during these years by difficulties in financing its regular programmes. In his 1983/84 Annual Report, the Commissioner-General expressed "grave concern about 1985 and beyond" and concluded, "I appeal again to the international community to ensure that the Agency is supplied with the resources it must have, if it is to carry out the will of the General Assembly."

Facing page:
With what is left on his back, a child flees the ruins of Ein el-Hilweh camp near Saida, south Lebanon, destroyed during the Israeli invasion of 1982.

Overleaf:
A ruined building, symbol of shattered lives. Weeks of fierce fighting in and around Beirut camps caused thousands of people to flee to safer areas. UNRWA distributed food rations and other necessities to the displaced refugees in Beirut, Saida and Tyre.

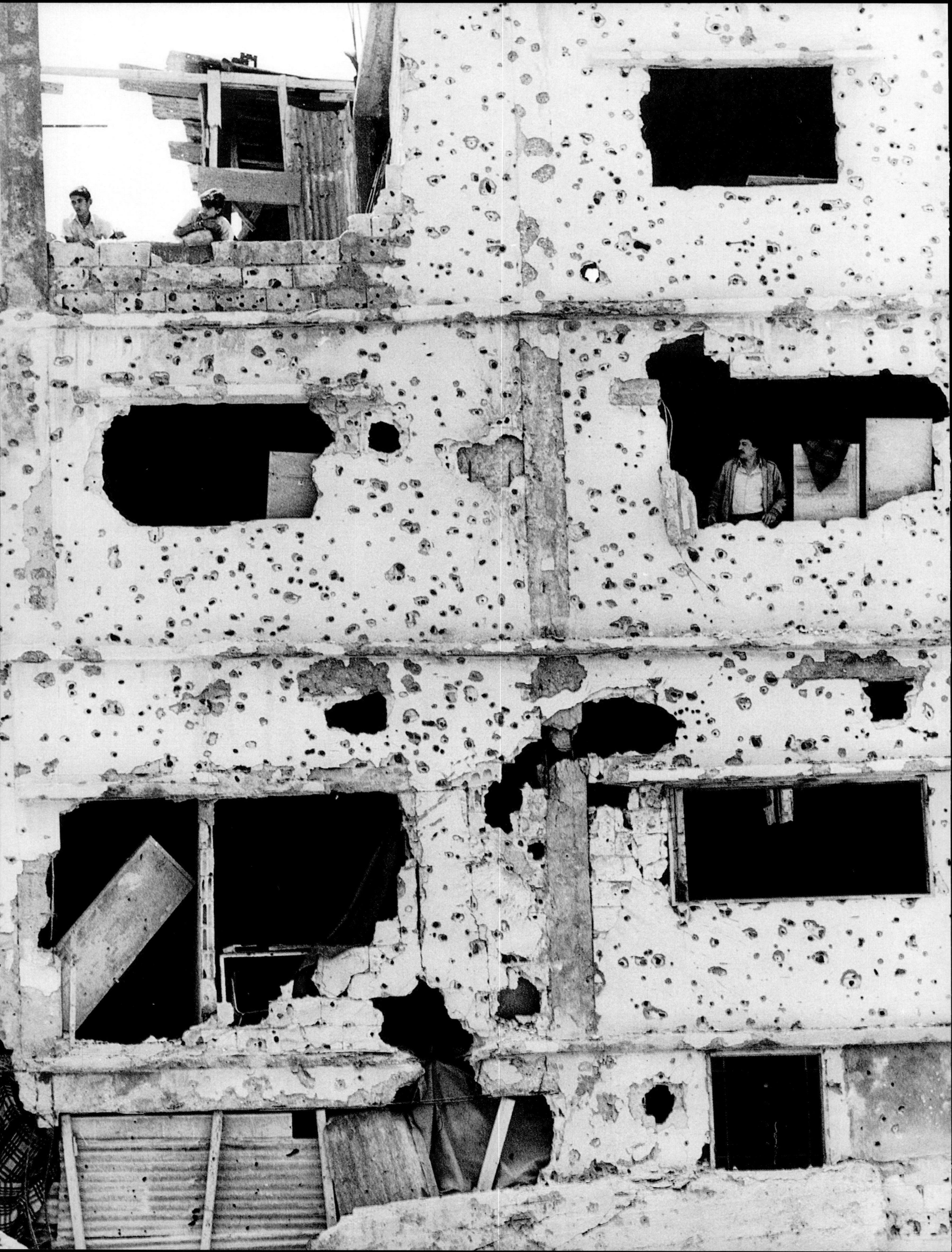

Chronology

	Israel invades Lebanon on 6 June.	**1982**
	UNRWA launches massive emergency relief programme.	
	General distribution of rations discontinued by UNRWA in all fields except Lebanon. Replaced by Special Hardship Case programme for neediest refugees.	
	Massacre at Sabra and Shatila.	
	Israel withdraws from Sinai Peninsula. Reinstatement of international border leaves thousands of Palestine refugees on the Egyptian side of Rafah.	
	Most normal Agency operations in Lebanon restored by end 1982.	
	UNRWA appeals for $ 13 million to rebuild refugee shelters, camp roads and drains and Agency facilities.	**1983**
	"Camps war" erupts, displacing 18,000 in Beirut.	**1985**
	Intra-Palestinian fighting in Tripoli area.	
	Heavy fighting in and around Beirut camps. Israeli air raids on camps in south Lebanon.	**1986**
	Refugee population surpasses 2 million, enrolment at UNRWA's 635 schools reaches 349,200 pupils, training centres accommodate 4,808 students, and clinics handle over 4 million patient visits during the year.	

Running for cover. Palestine refugee children and their teacher dash from classrooms to the safety of a bomb shelter as planes approach Rashidieh camp near Tyre. Schooling was disrupted time and again during the turbulent years in Lebanon but UNRWA continued to provide education services whenever and wherever it could.

Fleeing to safety. Refugees risk their lives as they escape from the besieged Burj el-Barajneh camp in Beirut.

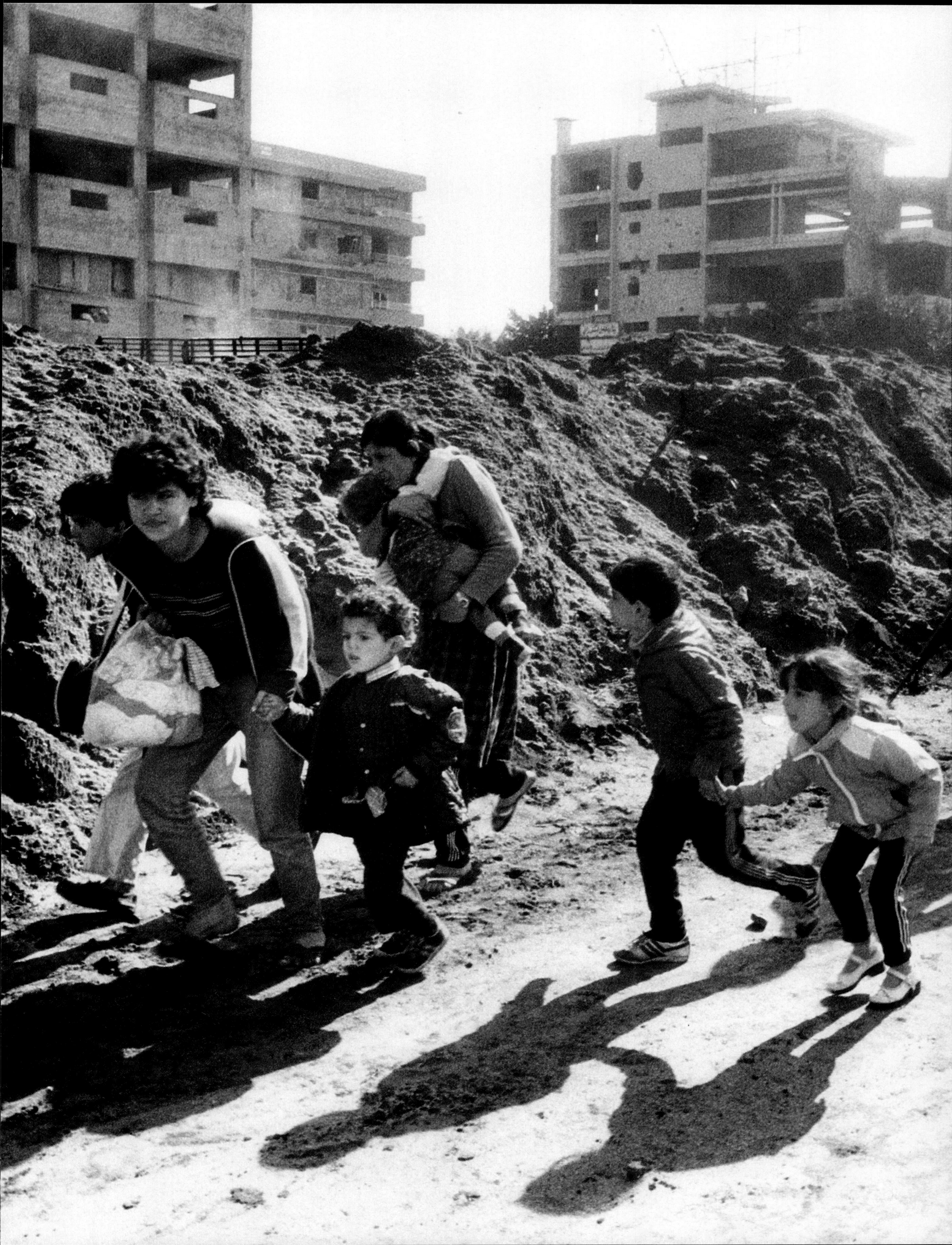

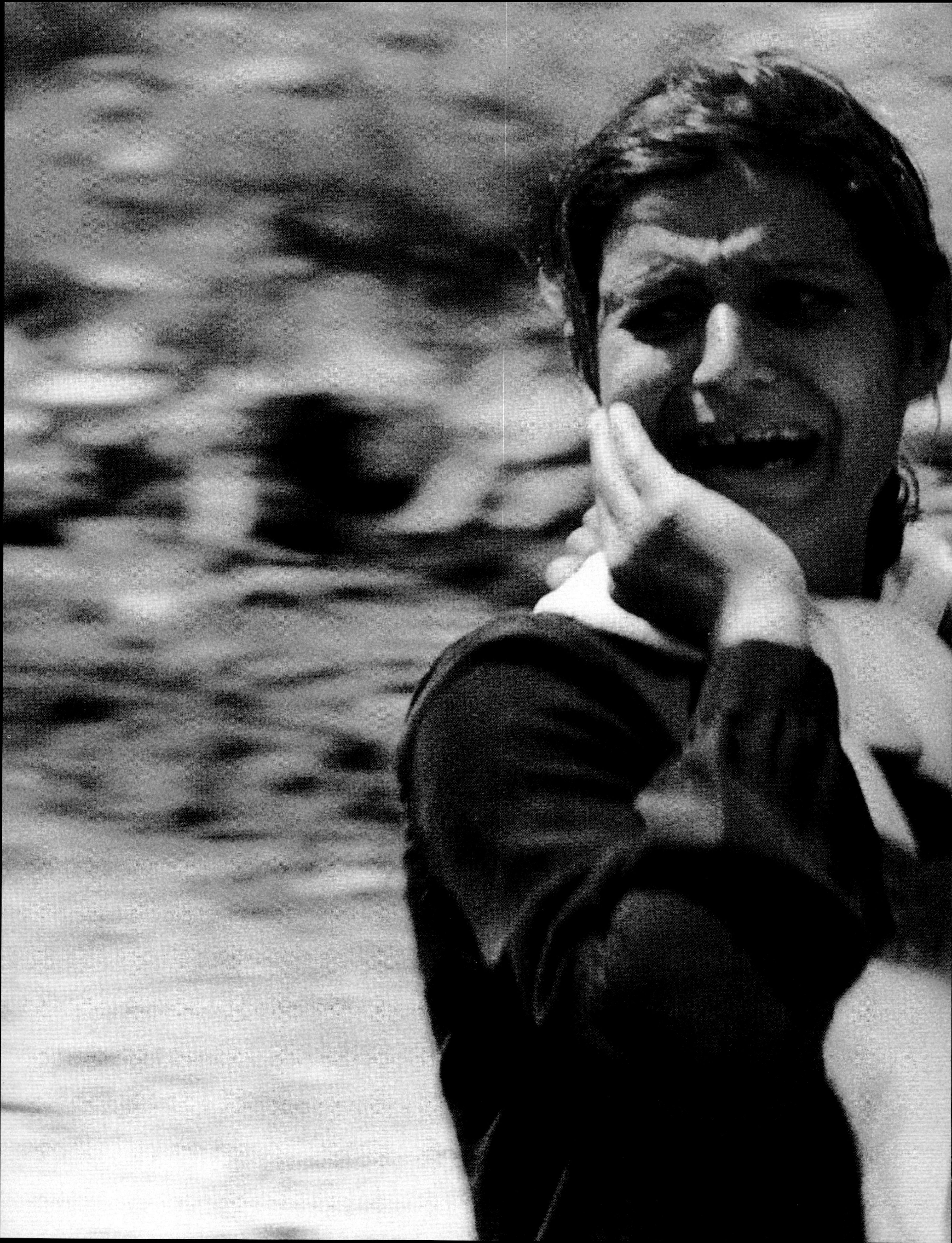

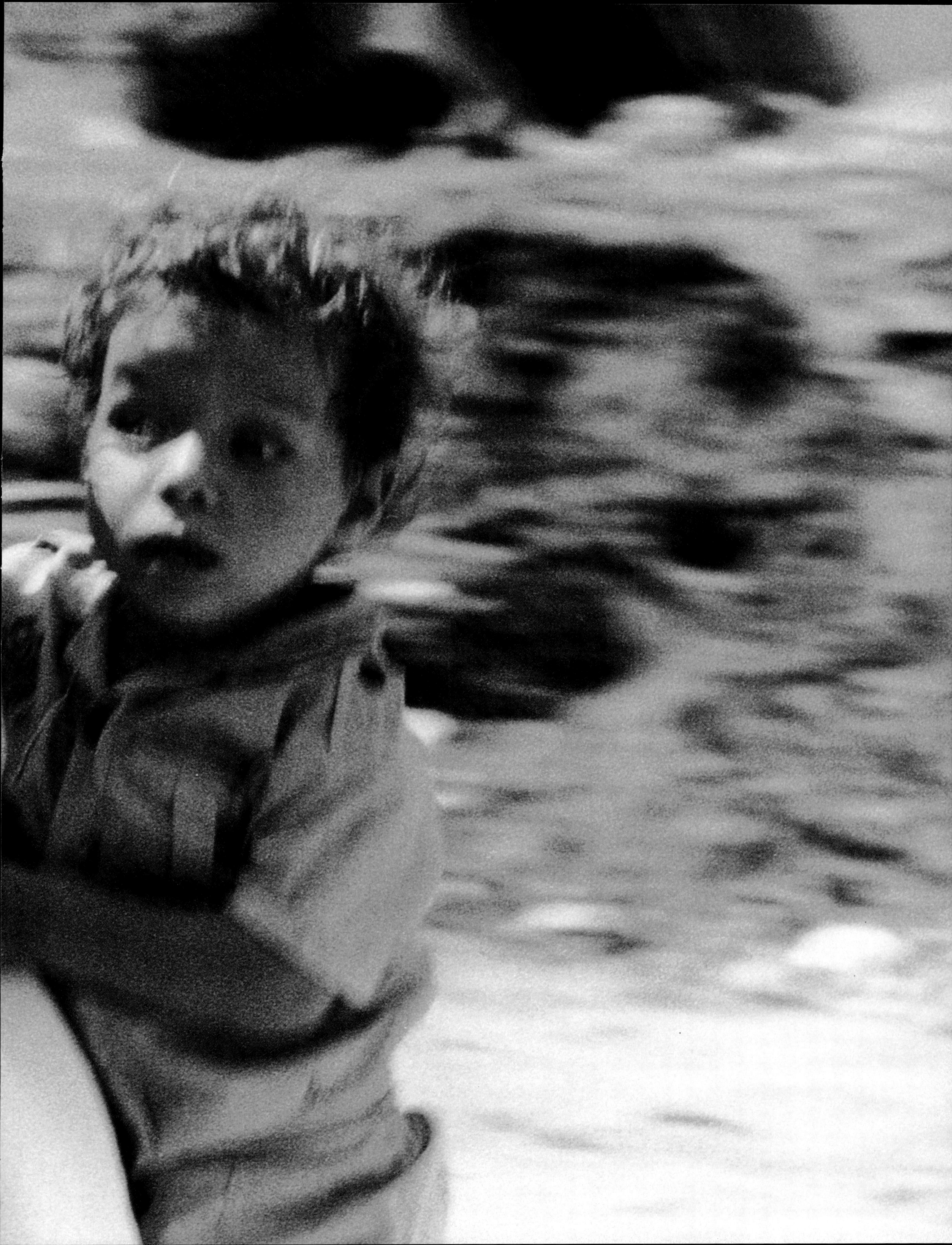

Previous pages:
Return to despair. A woman and her child return to Burj el-Barajneh camp, Beirut, after one of the attacks.

Shatila, Beirut, 20 September 1982. Hundreds of civilians were killed in the Sabra and Shatila districts of Beirut.

An UNRWA school in Burj Hamoud, Beirut, destroyed during civil unrest.

Door to nowhere. A Palestine refugee woman at the entrance of her bombed house in Burj el-Barajneh camp near Beirut in 1982.

An UNRWA relief convoy manages to reach the besieged Shatila district, Beirut, to distribute emergency food and urgently-needed medical supplies.

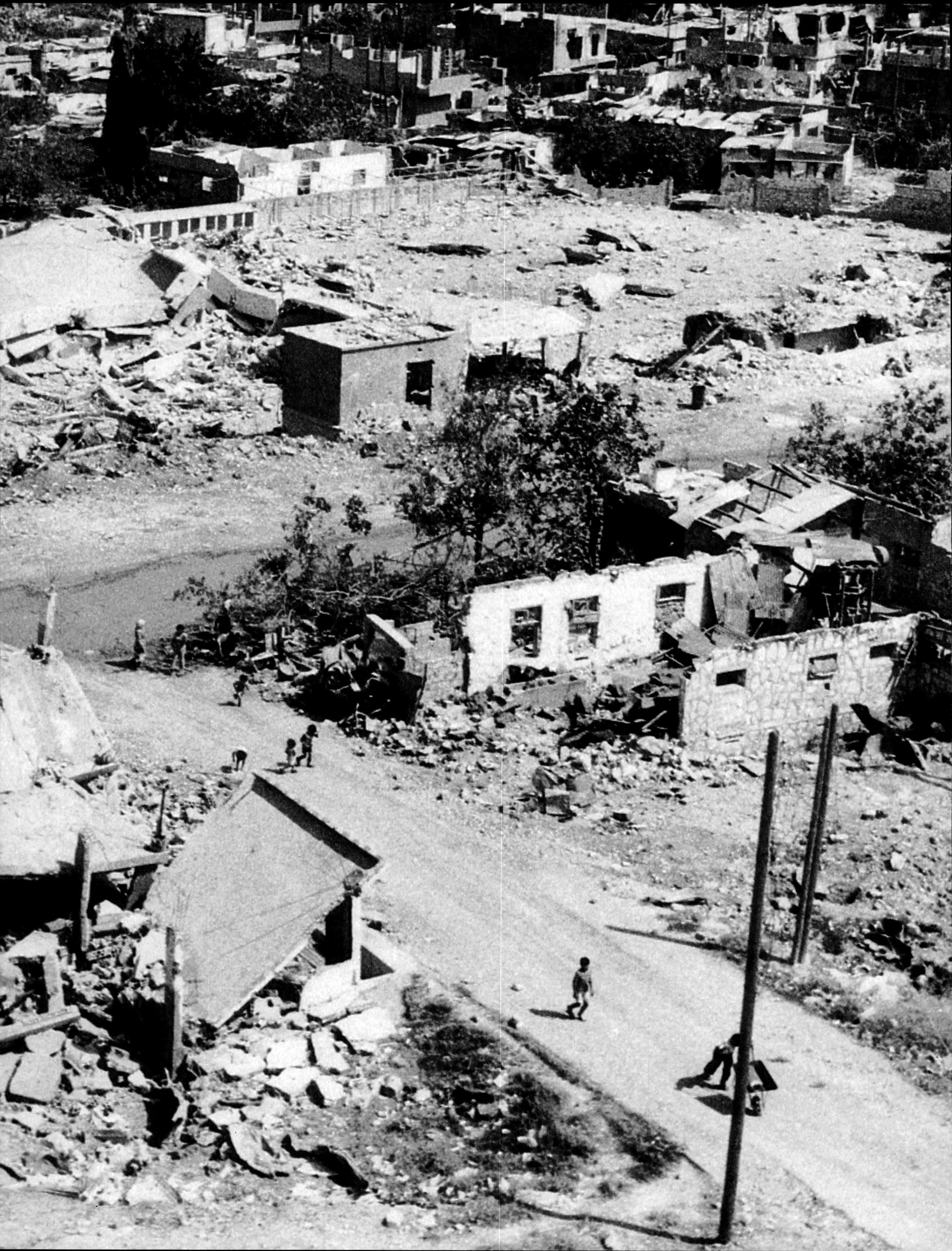

Learning goes on among the ruins of an UNRWA school in Shatila camp, Beirut.

A bullet-riddled sign over the UNRWA office in Burj el-Barajneh camp.

Reconstruction. Refugees whose homes were destroyed in Ein el-Hilweh camp, Saida, refused to live in tents again and began to repair and rebuild their homes under a self-help housing repair programme sponsored by UNRWA.

Facing page:
Many UNRWA buildings were destroyed as a result of the 1982 Israeli invasion of Lebanon. This school used to serve a community of 25,000 Palestine refugees in Ein el-Hilweh camp, Saida.

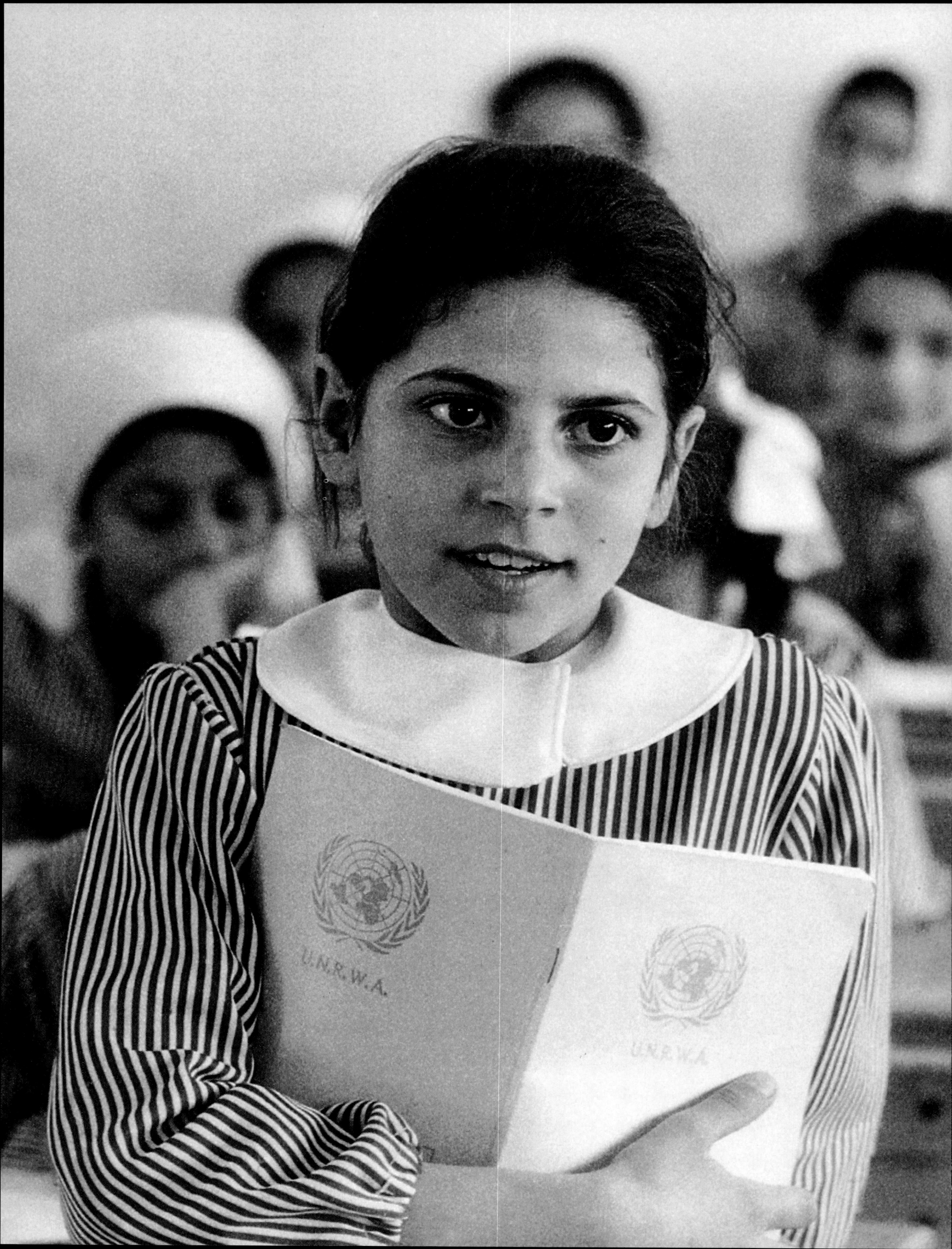
U.N.R.W.A.
U.N.R.W.A.

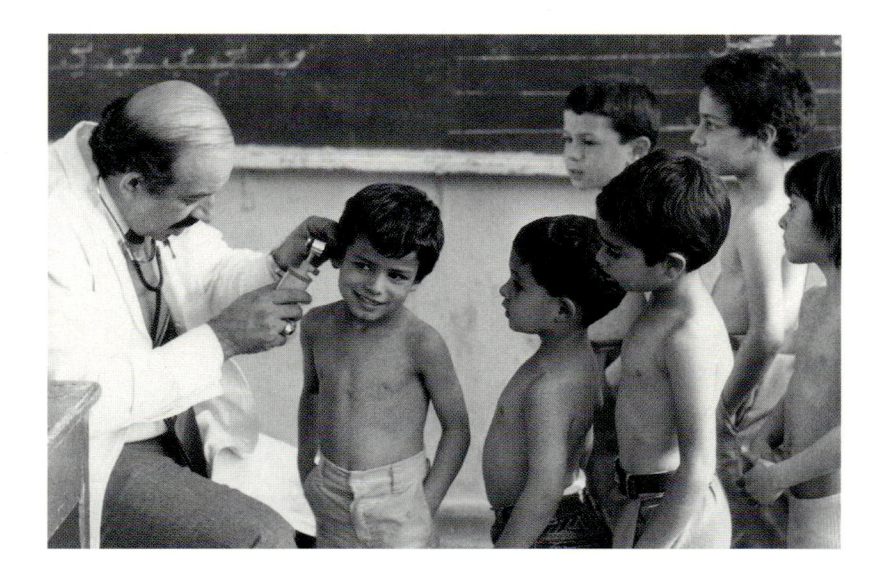

Keeping healthy. UNRWA's school health programme is one part of the preventive measures taken by the Agency to look after the health of hundreds of thousands of children at its schools.

Palestine refugee women learn alongside their male colleagues in an engineering course at UNRWA's Wadi Seer vocational training centre. Thousands of men and women have graduated from the centre since it opened in 1960.

A refugee girl works alongside the boys on a self-help project to improve the environment in Baqa'a camp, Jordan. Refugees have taken part in many self-help projects organized by UNRWA, re-roofing or rebuilding their shelters as well as setting up their own businesses using an initial loan from the Agency.

Facing page:
A schoolgirl in Jabalia camp in the Gaza Strip. Today nearly half of the Agency's budget is devoted to education. Girls account for 49 per cent of the student population.

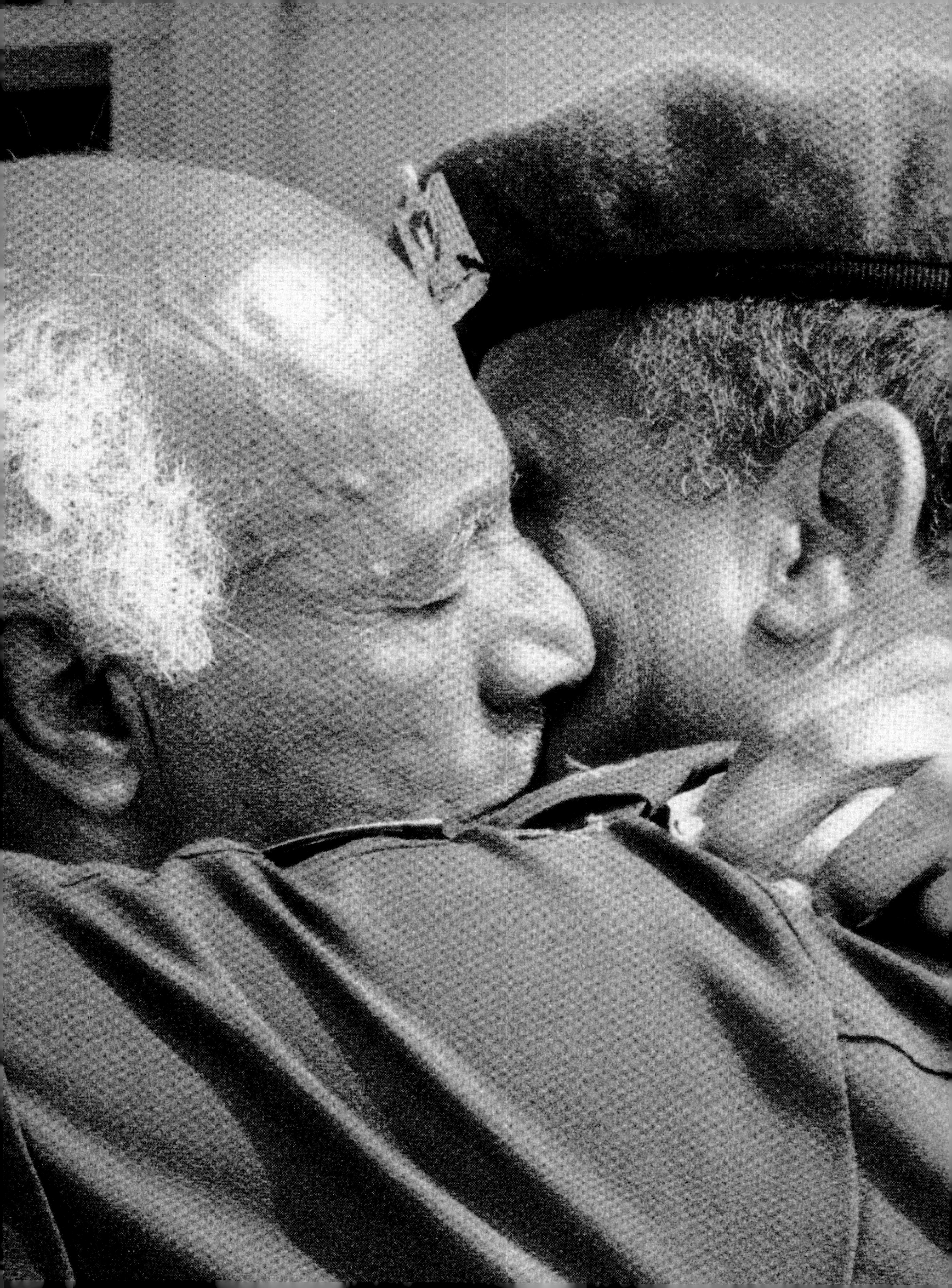

"The proudest moment of UNRWA will be when the refugee problem is resolved..."

87-95

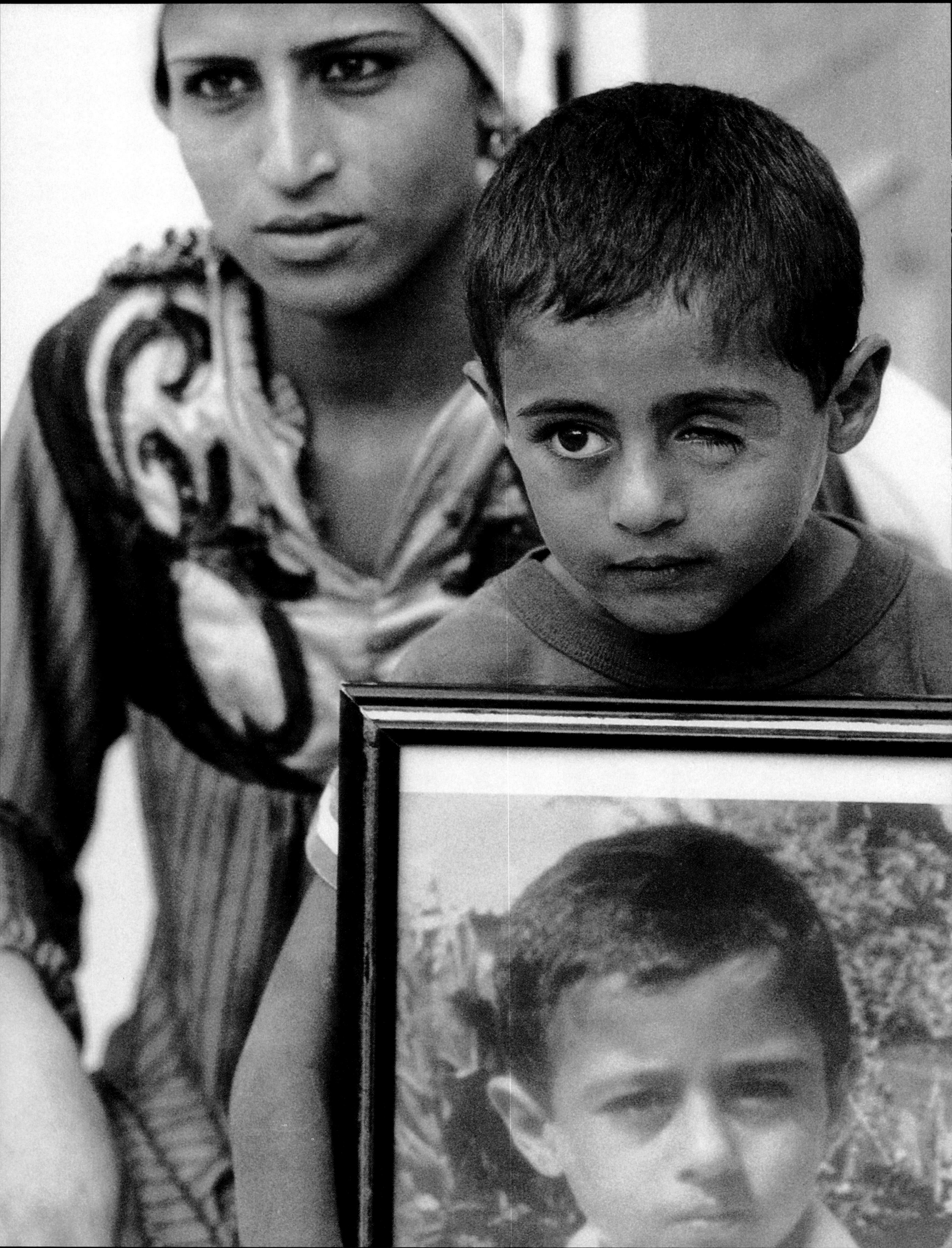

As early as August 1986, UNRWA was warning of deteriorating conditions in the occupied territory, especially Gaza. "There is a serious shortage of adequate housing and increasing numbers of refugees are finding it difficult to obtain employment. There is a growing sense of despair and hopelessness among the refugees...", said the Commissioner-General in his 1985/86 Annual Report.

In December 1987, clashes between Israeli security forces and Palestinians in Jabalia camp quickly spread throughout the Gaza Strip and to the West Bank. Within the month, more than 20 Palestinians had been killed and dozens wounded in confrontations with Israeli troops.

The authorities used a variety of measures to try to quell the uprising, or *intifadah*, as it was called in Arabic. These measures included travel restrictions, curfews, administrative detentions, expulsions and demolition or sealing of houses, as well as the use of beatings, tear gas, rubber bullets and live ammunition. The casualty toll grew, but so did resistance.

As socio-economic development in the occupied territory had been negligible for over two decades, Palestinians had had to rely heavily on work in Israel for their sustenance. Prior to the *intifadah*, up to 130,000 workers had crossed into Israel each day. Strikes and prolonged curfews kept workers at home, began to bite into savings held by refugees and to ravage an already deteriorating economy.

UNRWA was now faced with the continuation of its emergency operations in Lebanon, while having to deal with the new circumstances in the West Bank and Gaza Strip. Responding to a request from the UN Secretary-General, UNRWA began to draw up plans for improving refugee living conditions in the longer term as well as extending temporary humanitarian assistance to non-refugees, when needed.

As confrontations intensified and the response by the Israeli authorities hardened, UNRWA undertook emergency food distributions and opened 24-hour emergency clinics to treat the injured. Through its Refugee Affairs Officer (RAO) programme, the Agency aimed to maintain an international presence at scenes of confrontation in the occupied territory.

As a result of curfews, enforced closures and locally organized strikes, UNRWA's elementary and preparatory schools lost up to 40 per cent of teaching time during the *intifadah*. The Agency's vocational training centres were also closed for long periods.

The large number of Israeli settlements and settlers in both the West Bank and the Gaza Strip was another irritant to Palestinians. Not only were settlements taking land for housing and security, but they were also taking massive amounts of water, hurting Palestinian agriculture and leading to the degradation of already scarce water supplies in the Gaza Strip.

The Gulf crisis of 1990/91 was a severe setback to Palestinians throughout the region. Kuwait's Palestinian population was reduced to a tenth of its previous total. Most of those who left returned to Jordan, where UNRWA joined an international relief effort to provide health care and food. Thousands of children were provided places in UNRWA schools.

The effect of this new crisis on the residents of the West Bank and Gaza Strip was devastating. Jobs in the Gulf area dried up for Palestinians. Remittances from family members in the Gulf ceased. The Israeli Authorities imposed a six-week curfew on all of the Gaza Strip and most of the West Bank, including refugee camps, in early 1991. UNRWA again initiated emergency food distribution for refugees and non-refugees alike.

In March 1991, UNRWA expanded the scope of its income-generation programmes by establishing revolving loan funds in the West Bank and Gaza. These loans have helped to create or expand over 250 small enterprises. In 1992, a special environmental health programme was created to plan and coordinate efforts to improve the physical environment of refugee camps by installing sewerage and drainage systems.

The civil conflict in Lebanon slowly drew to a close. By mid-1991 a newly-formed government of reconciliation had taken office, gradually extending its authority throughout the country. UNRWA continued to provide assistance to the thousands of displaced Palestinians in Lebanon. Violence continued to plague the south, however.

In October 1991, the Madrid Conference, which Palestinians attended as part of the Jordanian delegation, raised some hope for a solution to the Middle East conflict. But living conditions in the occupied territory continued their downward spiral. Between July 1992 and June 1993, the Gaza Strip was sealed off at various times for a total of four months, while the West Bank was closed for shorter periods. Once again, UNRWA had to undertake emergency food distributions to Palestinians in both areas.

Most of 1993 was a dismal year for residents of the West Bank and Gaza. Some 13,000 Palestinians were in detention. Closures deprived workers of an estimated $ 2.75 million a day in wages, a figure representing over one-third of West Bank GNP and half of Gaza GNP. Exports of farm produce were hindered by administrative and security measures which caused costs of production and transport to rise above marked prices.

Suddenly - and unexpectedly - in September 1993, the Government of Israel and the Palestine Liberation Organization signed the Declaration of Principles which set the stage for the granting of self-rule in the Gaza Strip and the Jericho Area and the redeployment of Israeli forces.

As developments unfolded, UNRWA began to prepare a programme to support the peace process in the changed environment which would emerge in the self-rule areas.

Facing page:
Maimed for life. Nidal, a six-year-old Palestine refugee, lost an eye when hit by a rubber bullet fired by Israeli forces in May 1993. Over 1,000 Palestinians were killed and tens of thousands injured during the *intifadah*.

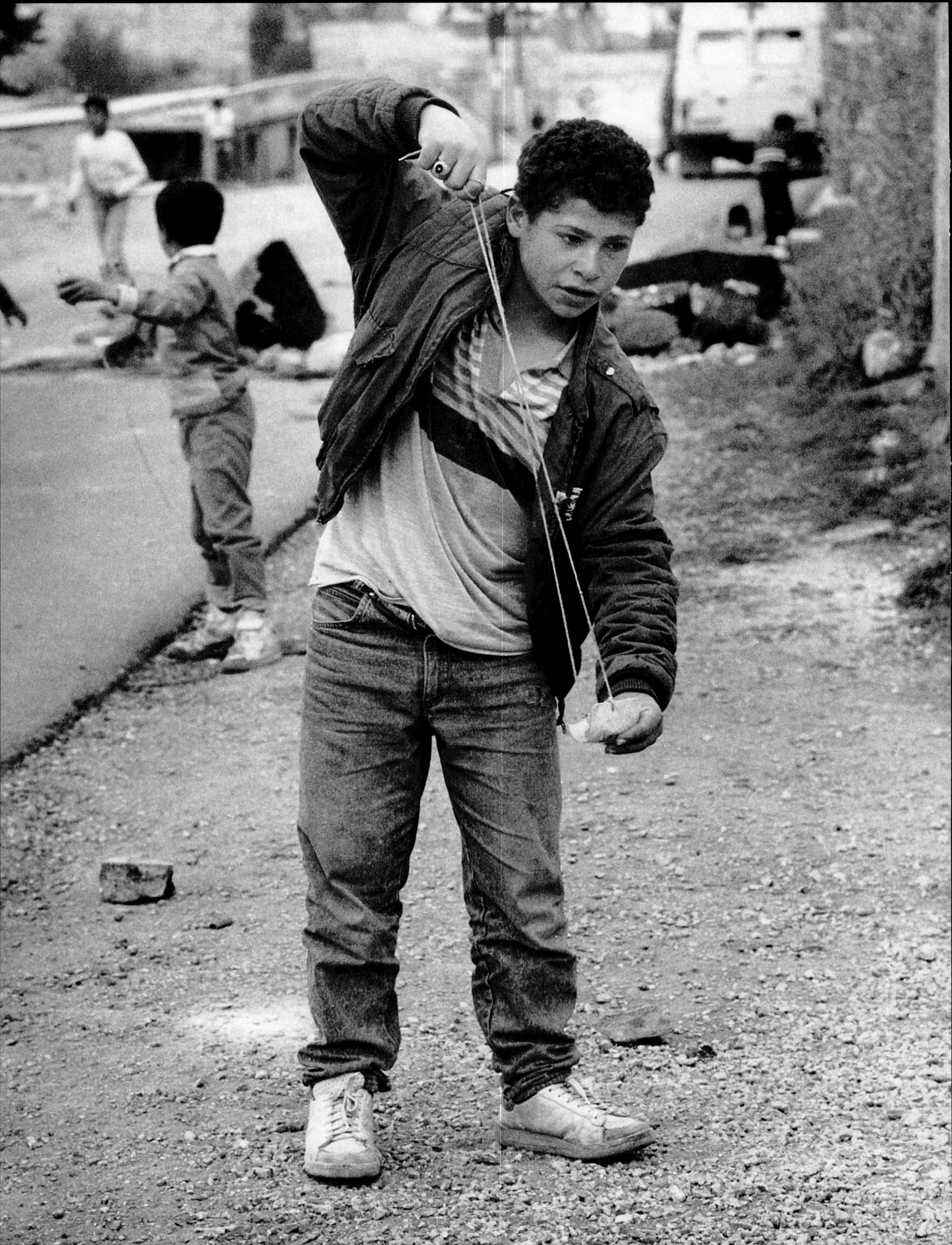

In October 1993, UNRWA unveiled its Peace Implementation Programme (PIP) for infrastructure development, income generation and job-creation. Donors responded quickly to UNRWA's plans for building schools, clinics and women's and youth activity centres; installing sewerage and drainage systems, and expanding income-generating projects. These plans were discussed and coordinated with the emerging Palestinian Authority, as well as other UN agencies involved in the development of the autonomous Palestinian areas. PIP activities were focused on the West Bank and Gaza Strip, but also included projects to improve the living conditions of Palestine refugees in Jordan, Lebanon and Syria.

The occupation continued with somewhat abating violence as talks between the Israelis and Palestinians inched along. The killing of 29 Palestinians worshipping at the Ibrahimi Mosque in Hebron by an Israeli settler in February 1994, briefly stalled the peace process. But both sides were committed to continue, and an agreement outlining transfer of authority in Gaza and Jericho as well as the redeployment of Israeli forces was signed in Cairo in May.

Gradually, the Israeli presence began to disappear from major population centres in the self-rule areas. The dusk to dawn curfew that had been in force in the Gaza Strip was no more. Citizens of Gaza and Jericho rejoiced in the streets as the Israeli army pulled out jeeps and dismantled installations.

The first units of Palestinian police arrived in late May and in June, and transfer of authority began. The policemen, some who had never been in Palestine, were mobbed by joyful Palestinians in Gaza who saw them as the first tangible evidence of the peace process.

On 1 July, PLO Chairman Yasser Arafat arrived in Gaza and quickly set up the Palestinian Authority to administer the fields of jurisdiction which had been agreed on in Cairo. UNRWA and the Palestinian Authority worked closely to harmonize their respective education, health and social services.

The economic situation for Palestinians nevertheless continued to worsen during 1994 and 1995 with repeated closures of both the Gaza Strip and West Bank after attacks on Israelis. Despite this, money was coming in, enabling the Palestinian Authority, UNRWA and other international organizations to begin implementing the construction of desperately needed roads, sewers, water systems, schools and health centres.

By mid-1995, under its Peace Implementation Programme, and with funds from a variety of sources, UNRWA had rebuilt or was in the process of repairing some 5,500 refugee shelters, 300 housing units for displaced refugees in Lebanon; had refurbished 28 UNRWA and Palestinian Authority schools and carried out repairs and upgrading on dozens more; and was constructing 31 new schools, 10 health units and nine women's programme centres, in addition to numerous other projects. The Agency was also building a 232-bed general hospital in the Gaza Strip with construction financing from the European Union as well as a college of nursing and health services. Major initiatives were under way to install internal sewerage systems in camps and municipalities in the West Bank, Gaza and Lebanon. UNRWA's ongoing income-generation programmes in all fields had provided loans to some 850 small enterprises, creating or saving hundreds of jobs and promoting self-reliance in refugee communities.

After 45 years of service to the Palestinian people and in the context of the new situation created by the peace process and the Declaration of Principles, UNRWA must begin to prepare for the time when its mission comes to an end.

Three major aspects of this process of devolution acquire great importance in this context. The Agency must prepare for the orderly transfer of its activities when an acceptable solution to the problem of the refugees has been found. It must also find the necessary human and financial resources to preserve its archives - invaluable historical documents of 45 years in the life of the Palestinian people. Finally, in cooperation with the international community, the Agency will have to devise and implement a satisfactory mechanism to carry on with its tasks during this last and most delicate period of its own existence.

In almost half a century of operations in the Middle East, UNRWA, by concentrating its efforts on Palestinian human resource development, has greatly contributed towards reinforcing the identity and community life of the Palestinian people who have suffered so much throughout the tragedy and conflict which has affected the region since the end of the Second World War.

For the first time since the Agency was established, it is now possible to forsee the end of its mission. As UNRWA's Comissioner-General, Ilter Türkmen stated: "The proudest moment for UNRWA will be when the refugee problem is resolved and we can finally say that all these people whom we have cared for throughout these 45 years, now have a different status. No longer a status of dependency, but a status of belonging somewhere."

Facing page:
War of the stones. A Palestinian boy prepares his sling for action in Jalazone camp, West Bank. Palestinians, most of them young people who had known nothing but years of occupation, hit back during the *intifadah*, using the most readily available weapons - stones.

Overleaf:
Intifadah: A pall of black smoke and the stench of burning tyres fill the air as Israeli soldiers move into Aida refugee camp, Bethlehem, February 1988. Similar scenes were repeated over and over again during the *intifadah* as Palestinians protested against the Israeli occupation.

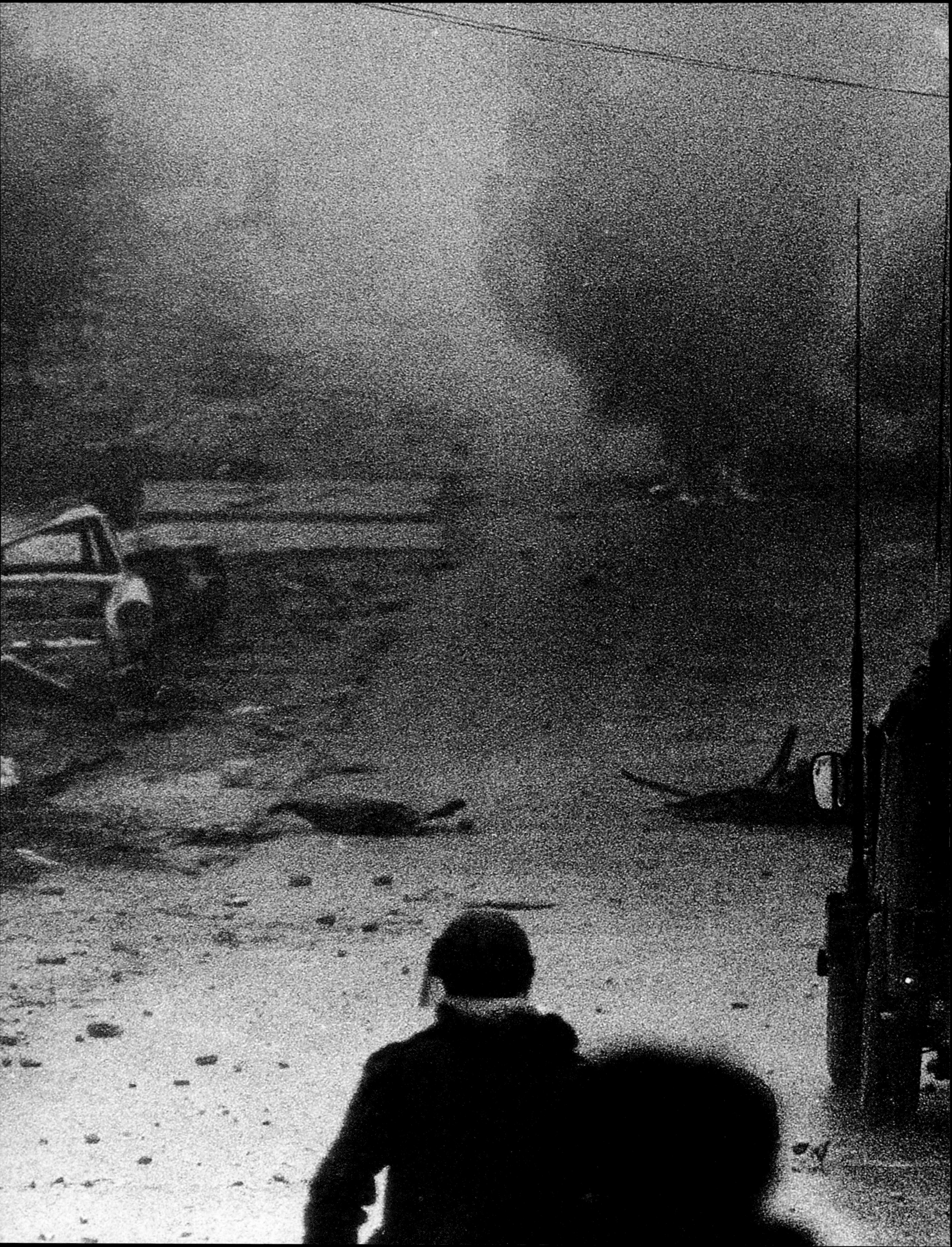

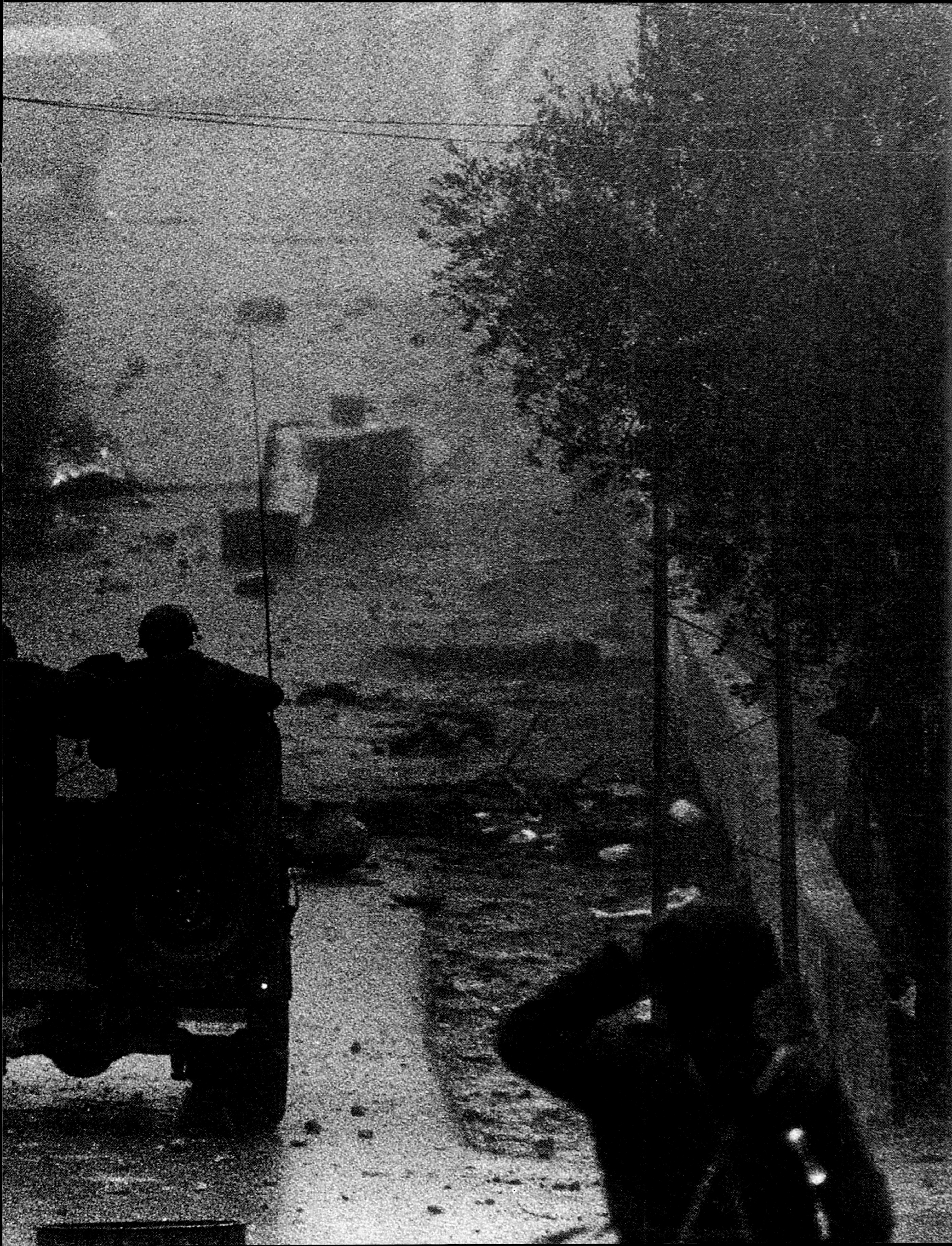

Chronology

1987   *Intifadah* begins in December

1988   UNRWA develops Expanded Programme of Assistance (EPA) in the West Bank and the Gaza Strip to deal with the socio-economic consequences of the *intifadah* and Israeli countermeasures.

1990   Political crisis in the Gulf. Over 300,000 Palestinians leave Kuwait, mainly to Jordan. UNRWA joins other international agencies in providing aid to the returnees.

1991   The Gulf war.

Six - week curfew on Gaza and large areas of the West Bank. UNRWA continues emergency operations and provides special food distribution.

UNRWA expands its income-generation programmes, setting up revolving loans funds in the West Bank and the Gaza Strip.

Lebanon's civil war comes to an end.

Madrid conference in October initiates the Middle East peace process.

1992   UNRWA establishes special environmental health programme in Gaza, and continues expanded activities in the occupied territory.

UNRWA's mandate extended to June 1996.

Refugee population reaches 2.7 million with UNRWA providing education to 392,000 pupils and vocational and technical training to 5,100 students; Agency health centres handle 6.1 million patient visits.

Declaration of Principles signed by Israel and the PLO. **1993**

UNRWA begins building 232-bed general hospital in Gaza.

Peace Implementation Programme launched by UNRWA to improve infrastructure and create jobs.

Decision made to move UNRWA Headquarters to the area **1994**
of operations.

29 Palestinians killed at Ibrahimi Mosque in Hebron.

Cairo Agreement, outlining redeployment of Israeli forces and transfer of authority, signed in May.

PLO Chairman Yasser Arafat arrives in Gaza on 1 July and establishes Palestinian Authority.

Inauguration of UNRWA Gaza College of Nursing. UNRWA begins construction of a new College of Nursing and Allied Health Sciences.

UNRWA launches second phase of Peace Implementation Programme.

UNRWA marks 45 years of service to Palestine refugees. **1995**
Number of Palestine refugees reaches 3.2 million.

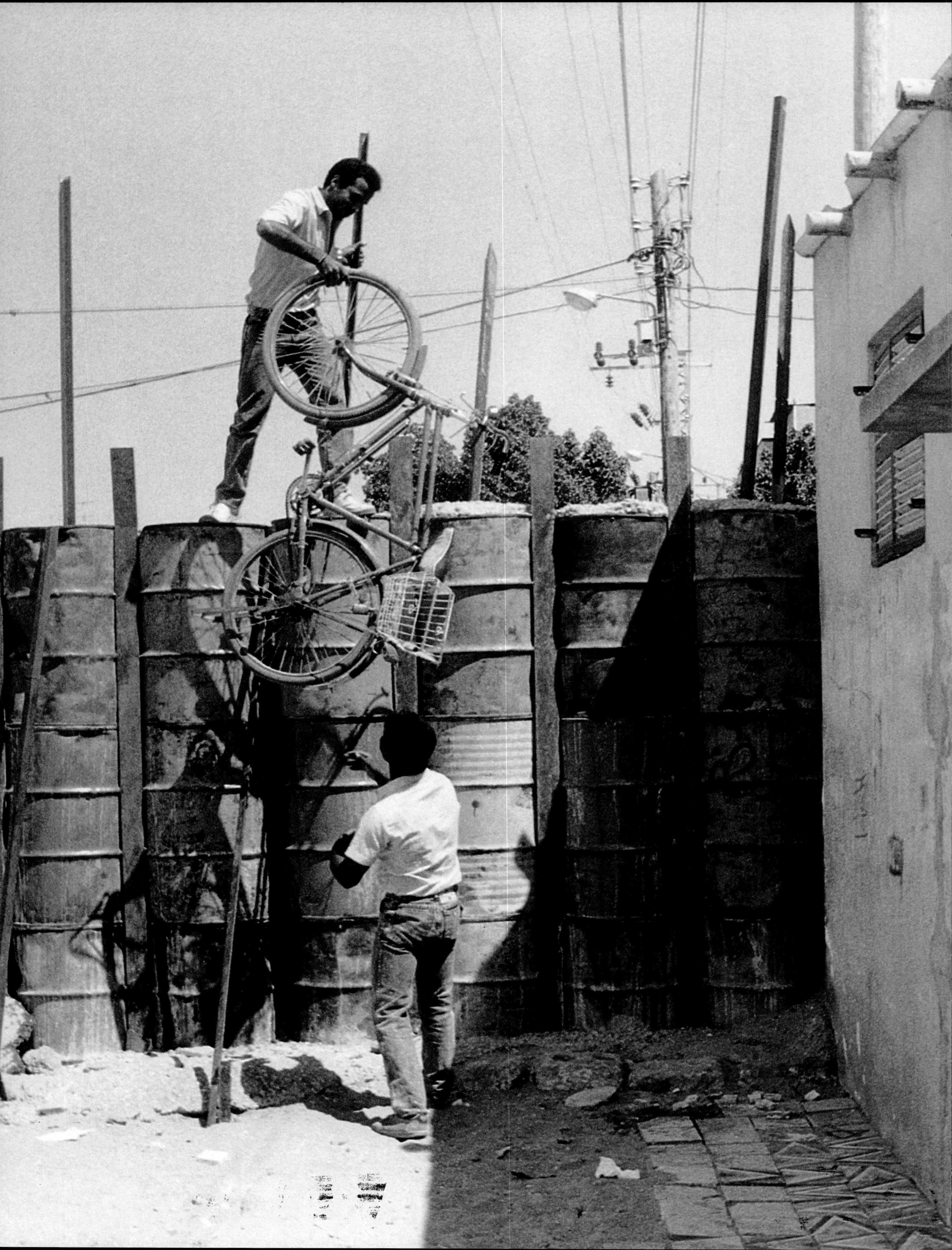

Israeli troops patrol the deserted streets of Gaza to enforce a curfew.

Palestinian girls vent their feelings against (unseen) troops in Gaza town during the *intifadah*, 1993.

My house: An UNRWA official shows the ruins of his house in Jalazone camp, West Bank, demolished by the Israeli authorities as a punitive measure two days after his release from nine months of detention without charge.

Facing page:
Palestinans have struggled to carry on a normal life under occupation. Here, at Beach camp, Gaza, a refugee lifts a bicycle over one of the many barricades put up by Israeli security forces to block camp entrances in Gaza and the West Bank during the uprising.

Palestinians in their shelter at Bureij refugee camp, Gaza, watching the historic signing of the May 1994 Cairo Agreement.

Celebrating change. Palestinians in Gaza celebrate the arrival of the Palestinian police force after the Cairo accord.

High spirits. May 1994: Raising the Palestinian flag above the fence of Gaza central police station on the day the Palestinian police moved in to replace Israeli soldiers.

Palestinian women celebrate the arrival of their own police force in Jericho in May 1994.

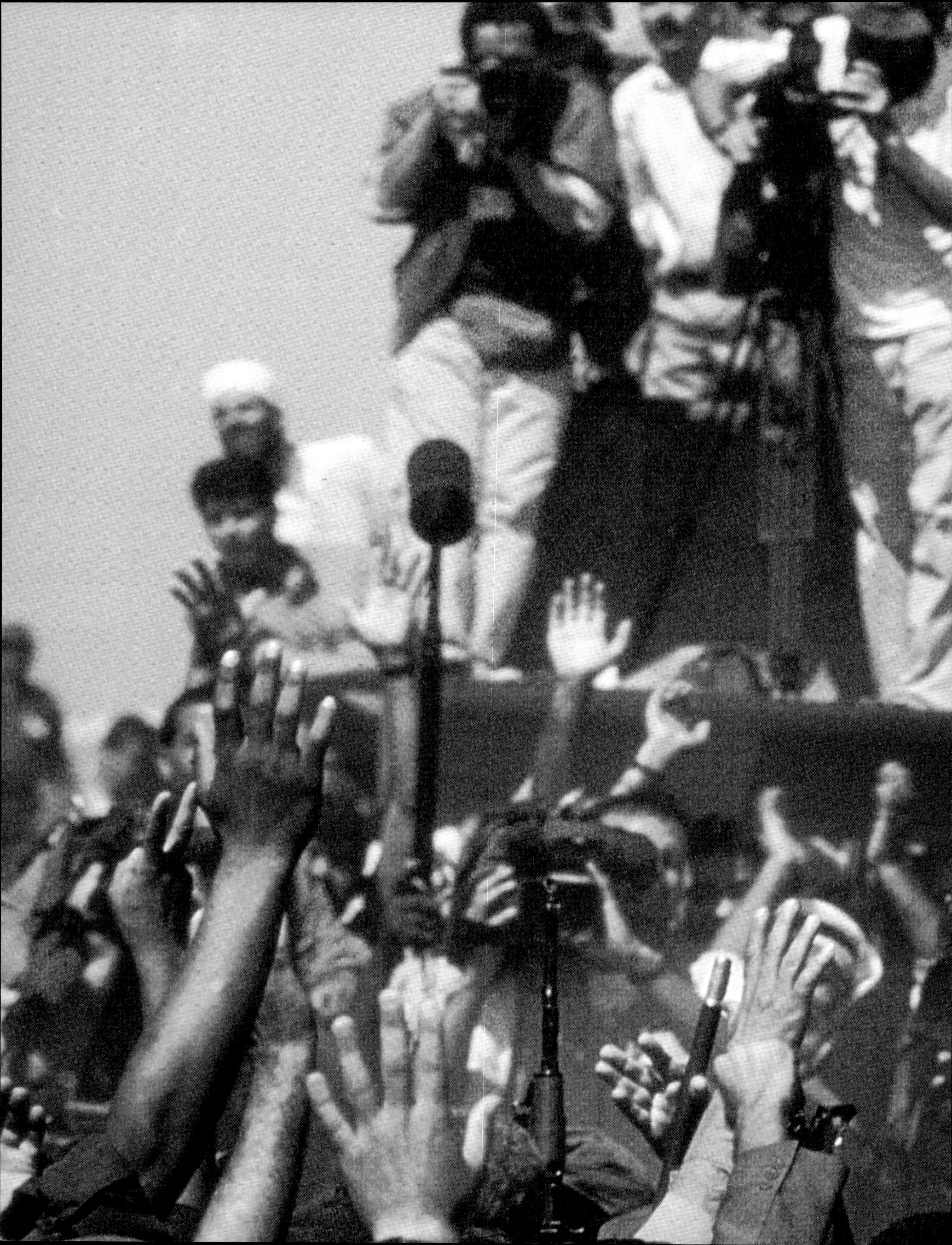

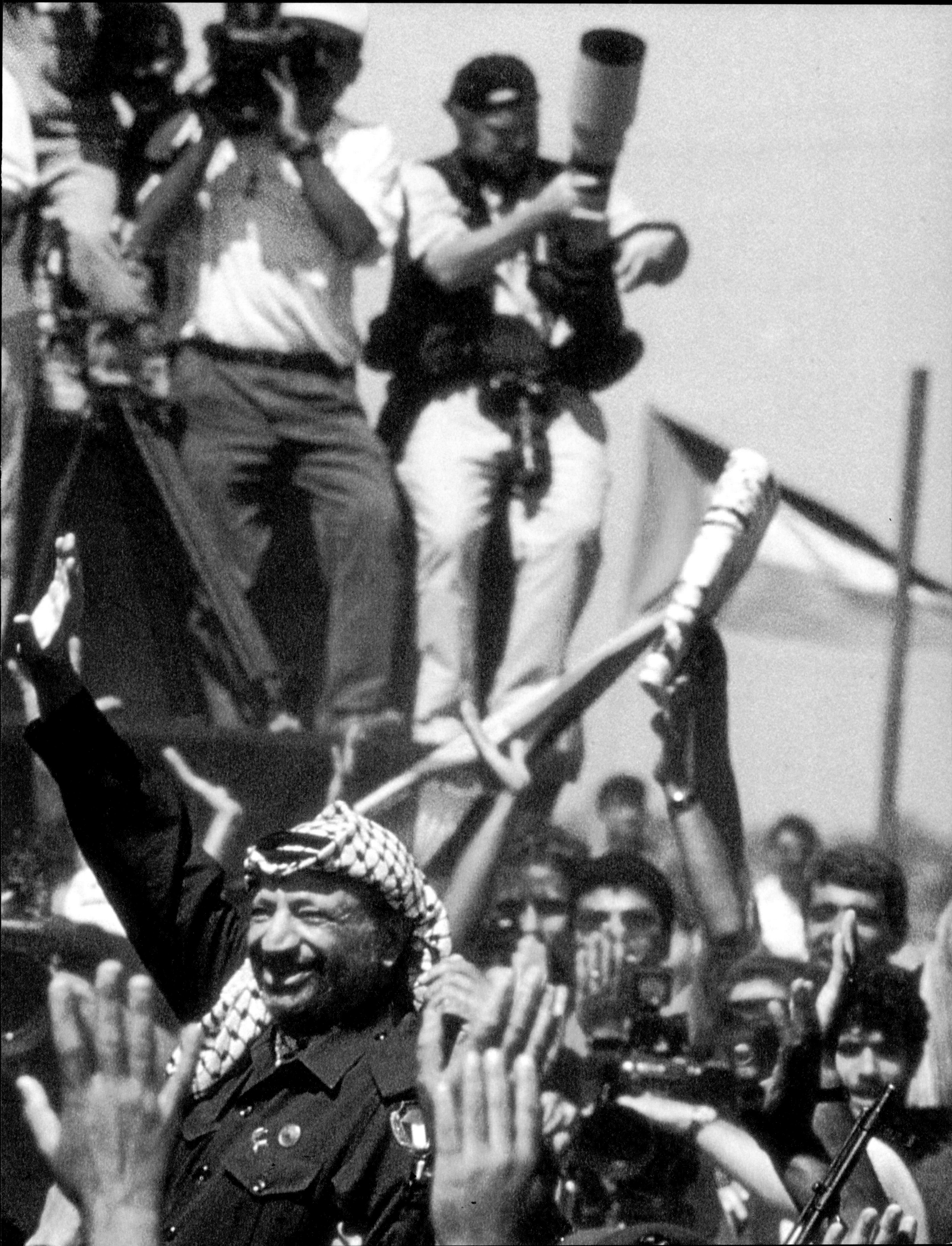

Previous pages:
Jubilation. 1 July 1994, Gaza. Hands go up in salute to Palestine Liberation Organization Chairman Yasser Arafat as he returns to Gaza, after years in exile.

Signs of changing times. A Palestinian policeman on duty at a new checkpoint in the Gaza Strip, summer 1994. For nearly 27 years prior to this, Gaza was policed by the Israeli forces.

Children catch up on a lost childhood, playing on barrels which previously blocked streets in Jabalia camp, just north of Gaza town. During the *intifadah*, the camp was the scene of almost daily clashes between young Palestinians and Israeli soldiers who kept watch from the observation tower.

Self-rule in action: a Palestinian policeman on traffic duty in Gaza town.

A family reunited. A Palestinian who has been released from an Israeli prison greets a relative. Thousands of similar reunions took place throughout Gaza and Jericho following the Cairo Agreement.

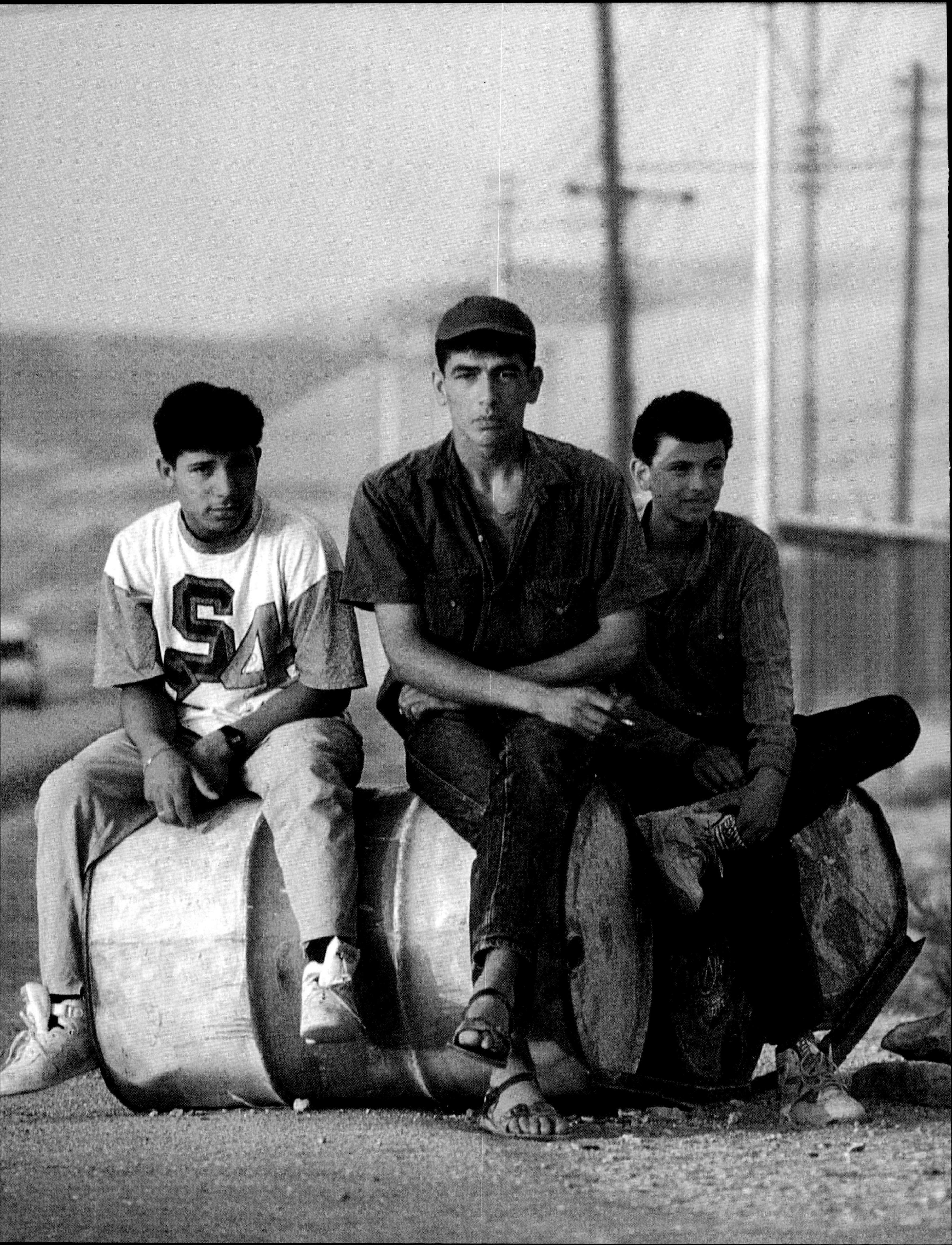

Well-earned harvest. Palestine refugee Mohammed Murshid is seen here with his family in front of the greenhouse they established in Tyre, south Lebanon with a loan from UNRWA.

Nurturing a living. Palestinians working in a greenhouse established with funds from UNRWA's income generation programme in the West Bank.

Lebanon: refugees' shelters being repaired or rebuilt with assistance from UNRWA. Under the Agency's Peace Implementation Programme (PIP), launched after the Declaration of Principles in 1993, more than 5,500 shelters have been repaired.

Facing page:
Young Palestinians from Aqabat Jabr camp near Jericho wait on the road for an early morning lift, hoping to find work. During the *intifadah*, lengthy closures of the occupied territory sent unemployment rocketing. UNRWA responded with a programme of poverty alleviation and income generation.

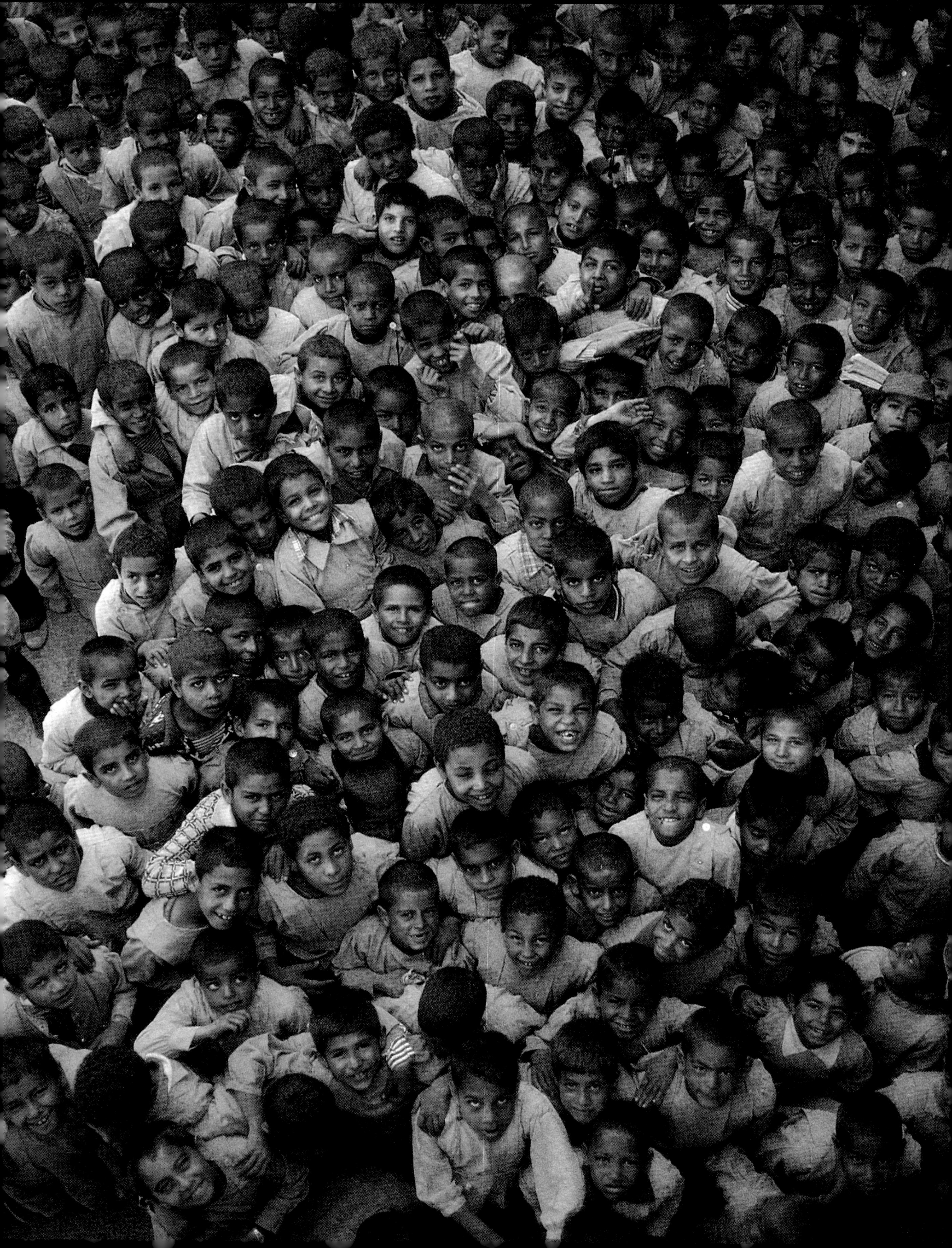

Young Palestine refugee men and women train in new technology at UNRWA's vocational training centre in Siblin, Lebanon, one of eight training centres run by UNRWA.

The new 232-bed general hospital being built by UNRWA in the Gaza Strip. Major construction projects are improving infrastructure and creating jobs for refugees.

An UNRWA environmental project in Gaza. Under PIP, UNRWA started projects to improve infrastructure, living conditions and job prospects for Palestine refugees.

Facing page:
Faces full of hope - children at an UNRWA school in Jaramana camp, Syria. Generations of Palestine refugee children have received their first years of education in UNRWA schools.

Overleaf:
A grandfather rests his hand - and hopes - on his grandson. Four generations of Palestine refugees still await a solution to their plight.

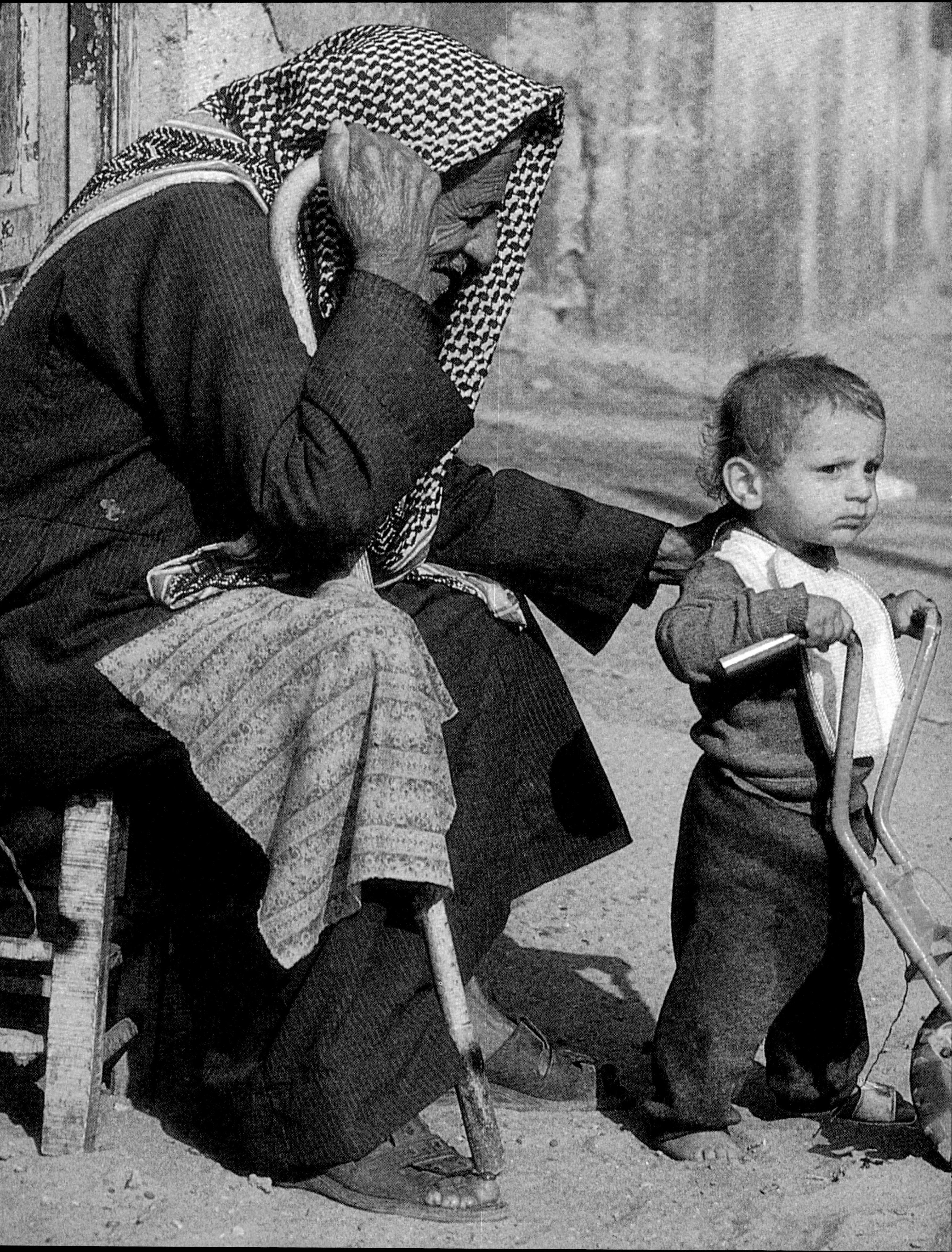

Credits

ACKNOWLEDGEMENTS:

UNRWA gratefully acknowledges the financial assistance received towards the production of this book from:

Finnish Refugee Council

Soka Gakkai International, Japan

United Nations Association of Sweden

Editorial and production team: Zuheir Abdullah, Ghazi Al-Hammal, Sommer Aweidah, Mohammed El-Haj, Lynn Failing, Annette Frick, Shawkat Hasan, Hayat Hayek, Marie Thérèse Kiriaky, Marianne Kounitson, Zaven Mazakian, Sami Mshasha´, Munir Nasr, Sandro Tucci, Jennifer Waller, Ron Wilkinson, Magdalena Winzig.

Photos from: The UNRWA photo library, Vienna, and the United Nations archives, New York.

UNRWA photos by: F. Audeh, Kay Brennan, Myrtle Winter Chaumeny, H. Haider, Shawkat Hasan, Jack Madvo, F. Mayer, Munir Nasr, George Nehmeh, Sandro Tucci, Odd Uhrbom.

Graphic design and print supervision: Johannes Niedermaier and Christian Treppel, OUT OF ORDER, Vienna, Austria

ISBN: 92-1-100709-7   UN Sales Number: GV.E. 95.0.26